The Productivity Imperative

About the series

The McKinsey Global Institute (MGI) was established in 1990 as an independent economics think tank within McKinsey & Company, the management consultancy, to conduct original research on critical economic issues. Its primary purpose is to provide insights and facts about developments in the global economy that will help business leaders and policymakers to make better decisions.

This anthology of articles published by MGI is part of a multi-volume set. Each volume presents conclusions drawn from MGI's principal research projects, in particular over the past five years, illuminating related themes.

The Productivity Imperative: Wealth and Poverty in the Global Economy

Articles in this volume show why and how the level of productivity in an economy—the ratio of output to input—is the key determinant of its rate of growth. In studies of numerous economies around the world, both developed and emerging, MGI has measured productivity levels sector by sector and analysed how they might be improved.

Driving Growth: Breaking Down
Barriers to Global Prosperity

This series book describes three barriers to productivity improvement that MGI has frequently encountered in its studies on productivity in individual countries.

Offshoring: Understanding
the Emerging Global Labor Market

This volume in this series of anthologies contains articles that estimate the likely extent of offshoring and how businesses and policymakers on both sides of this emerging global labor market can better manage the phenomenon. The key is not to obstruct offshoring, but instead to make sure that some of the resulting gains are directed towards those who lose out from it.

The Productivity Imperative

Wealth and Poverty
in the Global Economy

Edited by Diana Farrell,
McKinsey Global Institute

Harvard Business School Press
Boston, Massachusetts

Copyright 2006 McKinsey & Company, Inc. United States.

All rights reserved

Printed in the United States of America

10 09 08 07 06   5 4 3 2 1

No part of this publication may be reproduced, stored in or introduced
into a retrieval system, or transmitted, in any form, or by any means
(electronic, mechanical, photocopying, recording, or otherwise), without
the prior permission of the publisher. Requests for permission should be
directed to permissions@hbsp.harvard.edu, or mailed to Permissions,
Harvard Business School Publishing, 60 Harvard Way, Boston,
Massachusetts 02163.

ISBN 10: 1-4221-1026-5
ISBN 13: 978-1-4221-1026-3
Library of Congress Cataloging in Publication Data is forthcoming.

The paper used in this publication meets the minimum requirements of the
American National Standard for Information Sciences—Permanence of
Paper for Printed Library Materials, ANSI Z39.48-1992.

Contents

The productivity imperative

Economists have long considered the problem of how to increase an economy's growth rate. Finding a solution is crucial, given the widening gulf between the world's richest and poorest nations. Unacceptable in human terms, this disparity is fuelling social tensions and flows of economic migrants on a scale that both rich and poor countries find hard to manage. How to rekindle growth is also a critical question for that group of recently developed economies whose growth rates seem to have stalled, as it is for those mature economies in Europe struggling to meet voters' expectations of continually rising prosperity.

In search of answers, the McKinsey Global Institute (MGI) has conducted research over the past 16 years on the structure and evolution of nearly twenty national economies at all levels of development—rich, poor, and in between. Unlike some academic economists, with only aggregate data to work on, MGI has had the opportunity to study how these economies operate at the microeconomic level, sector by sector, across a range spanning nearly 30 sectors.

This scrutiny of economies from the bottom up, so to speak, has revealed that there is one certain way to accelerate GDP growth: increase levels of labor productivity among individual firms. We also conclude that the most effective way for policy-makers to help individual firms increase their productivity is to create the conditions in each industry sector for fierce but fair competition between all participating firms.

These two conclusions sound simple, but they are immensely powerful. They imply that an economy can achieve rapid growth before reaching an economy-wide "first world" level of infra-structure, capital formation, technology, education or health, contrary to the views of some economists. That means policy-makers in any economy can start to speed its growth straight away by enacting regulations that support more competition in each sector, and removing factors obstructing competition. Moreover, policymakers need not increase competitive intensity across the whole economy all at once to see a result: they can ap-proach the task sector by sector, a more manageable prospect.

The outcome of rising labor productivity will be not only a bigger national income but also higher employment, as long as regulations allow the labor market to respond to changes in de-mand. Although individual firms may become more productive by adopting less labor intensive processes and shedding staff, the combined impact of ploughing their larger surpluses back into the economy will be higher aggregate demand, in turn triggering the creation of more new jobs. The US economy, with one of the world's highest levels of overall labor productivity, also has a relatively low rate of unemployment.

This anthology includes 11 MGI articles that demonstrate how increasing productivity at the sector level results in higher economic growth. They also illustrate how poor regulations, often well-intentioned, can hold back growth by impeding fair competition between enterprises. The articles are grouped in two sections:

1. How competition promotes economic growth

The two articles in this section explain the relationships between GDP growth, increasing productivity, competition, and regulation. *The power of productivity,* by MGI's founding director Bill Lewis, shows how the income level of a country is determined, above all, by the productivity of its largest industries, and how competition spurs companies to find new ways to produce more output for less input. The surplus earned by the more innovative and thus more productive companies helps them to expand and take market share from less productive ones. These must also become more efficient, or else go out of business. Either way, consumers gain, as the winning companies offer better goods at lower prices. As well as lowering prices, more productive companies may use their surplus to expand production, and so create more jobs directly, or to reward shareholders with higher returns and workers with higher wages. But however they spend their productivity bonus, it will make the economy grow.

Market economies must have some kinds of regulation to function properly. For instance, property rights must be protected and monopolies prevented to ensure that competition produces outcomes that benefit society. However, regulators—often with the best of intentions—frequently make rules that go beyond what is necessary to support competition. Rules aimed at protecting one group's interests—industrial workers, for example—may disadvantage less well represented groups, like the unemployed. *Regulation that's good for competition* sets out practical guidelines for deciding the content and scope of regulatory frameworks that will encourage free and fair market competition without unfortunate and growth-hindering consequences.

2. The productivity imperative at work

Articles in this section present findings from a selection of MGI's country studies. All of them give examples of how measures to increase competitive intensity—especially regulatory reforms—within an industrial sector have resulted in rising levels of sector productivity, and vice versa.

First published in 2002, when the US economy was hit by the aftermath of the high-tech bust and September 11th, *What's right with the US economy* argued that competitive intensity in key sectors of the US economy was sufficient to ensure that overall productivity in the economy would continue rising rapidly, although maybe not quite as fast as in recent years. Our position was based on a year-long MGI study of US productivity between 1995 and 2000, which found that competition was more responsible than just IT investments for the "new economy" that emerged in the United States over the period. Later sector productivity figures for the United States (discussed in a sidebar to this article published in 2006) showed this position was valid.

There is hot debate over why labor productivity in France and Germany, after seeming set to catch up with levels in the United States, has fallen behind again. Many have argued that Europe's lower investment in IT and R&D is the cause, and that more government-supported research will fix the problem. *Reviving French and German productivity* shows that lower IT investment can explain only part of the growing gap. MGI research on six sectors—automotive, retail banking, retail trade, road freight, telecommunications, and utilities—in these countries shows that a raft of regulations have unnecessarily restricted competition in these sectors in France and Germany, holding back productivity growth.

During the seven years to 2006, Sweden's economy grew at an impressive average of 2.7 percent, after several decades of decline relative to its peers in Europe. *Sweden's golden opportunity* traces the impetus for that recovery to widespread deregulation and European Union membership, which heightened competition and spurred key private sector industries to become more productive. However, in sectors where competition did not intensify, notably the large public sector, levels of productivity appear worryingly low. Moreover, regulations restricting the labor market mean the private sector revival has not been accompanied by more new private sector jobs. This article sets out actions Sweden should take now to ensure the economy grows fast enough to maintain its acclaimed social provision in the future.

Turkey's economy is at a very different stage of development. Our 2003 research on that country, reported in *Turkey's quest for stable growth,* illustrates how regulations and business practices allowing firms with very low levels of productivity to survive prevent more productive companies in the same sector from winning the market share they deserve. Yet the more productive companies have the potential to contribute much greater value to the economy, as well as, ultimately, more and better jobs. Reforms to enable the modern, productive companies to thrive can raise employment substantially and put Turkey in a better position to join the EU.

Asia: the productivity imperative draws on earlier MGI studies in India, Japan, Korea, and Thailand to show that all four have some industries with exemplary levels of productivity, and others that are staggeringly inefficient. Their productive sectors are those that produce for export, and are thus subject to the forces of global competition. It is their domestic, non-tradable services, with no foreign rivals by definition, which have fallen behind. The challenge for policymakers is to simulate the competitive effects of trade in these less efficient sectors. Some argue that subjecting domestic sectors like food processing and construction to greater competition will erode their distinctive national character. But higher productivity is not synonymous with greater scale and uniformity, or the sacrifice of local tastes. The food processing industry in France, for instance, is 96 percent as productive as in the United States, while remaining distinctively French.

In *China and India: the race to growth,* three experts on these emerging giants give their views on which has the stronger approach to economic development. Drawing on MGI's work in China, my section points out that the question can only be answered sector by sector. In both countries, those sectors experiencing intense and well-regulated competition, such as the consumer electronics industry in China and automotive industry in India, are rapidly increasing labor productivity and growing their contribution to GDP. But both countries also have sectors where competition is far less intense—consumer electronics in India, and automotive in China—and performance less impressive. For both economies, raising productivity in those sectors that employ the most people, like agriculture and food retailing, will be the key to maintaining rapid growth and spreading its benefits more uniformly across their massive populations.

In 2001, MGI studied India's economy to understand whether it could grow even faster than the 6 percent a year it then achieved. Close examination of 13 industry sectors revealed the huge opportunities for accelerating growth described in *India: from emerging to surging.* By revising the mass of regulations constraining product markets, removing distortions in the market for land, and reducing the extent of state ownership in sectors where it added no value, MGI calculated that policymakers could increase the economy's growth rate by 4 percent a year and create 75 million new non-farming jobs.

A richer future for India was written shortly after the general election in 2004, when the majority appeared to have cast their vote against further economic liberalization. The article shows how more global competition and foreign direct investment in India's economy would lift a far greater number of people out of poverty and into paid work than a return to protectionism ever could.

While Brazil's policymakers have drawn praise for their success in tackling hyperinflation, the economy has yet to fulfill its high growth potential. *How Brazil can grow* reports the five remaining barriers to productivity improvement uncovered by MGI's most recent study there. The size of Brazil's informal economy is the most important. Informal enterprises that avoid taxes and ignore labor regulations gain a large but unearned cost advantage, which their formal competitors find it almost impossible to match through legal productivity improvement. Informal firms therefore "steal" market share from the firms with the potential to contribute most to the economy. The other important barriers to growth in Brazil are macroeconomic factors that hinder investment, inappropriate regulations, poor public services, and a weak infrastructure. The good news, however, is that tried and tested policies exist for tackling all five barriers.

—Diana Farrell
Director, McKinsey Global Institute

1

The power of productivity

William W. Lewis

IDEAS IN BRIEF

Economic progress depends on increasing productivity, which depends on undistorted competition. When government policies limit competition, even unintentionally, companies that are more efficient can't replace less efficient ones.

To understand why some countries are mired in poverty, it is necessary to look beyond broad macroeconomic policies, such as interest rates and budget deficits, and also consider the myriad zoning laws, investment regulations, tariffs, and tax codes that hold back the productivity of industries and thus a nation's prosperity.

Differences in the productivity of countries are attributed not to differences in labor or capital markets, but to the nature of competition in product markets.

After the Second World War, a vast array of international and national institutions—the United Nations, the World Bank, the International Monetary Fund, and a host of nongovernment and government aid organizations—was created to better the lot of the world's poor. Conventional wisdom came to hold that improvements in infrastructure, technology, capital markets, education, and health care would eliminate the stark distinctions between rich and poor nations.[1] Fifty years and billions of dollars later, this wisdom has proved wrong.

At the beginning of the 1990s, the Soviet Union's fall precipitated a new conventional wisdom. This "Washington consensus" focused heavily on macroeconomic policies, such as flexible exchange rates, low inflation, and government solvency, while also embracing microeconomic elements—for instance, price decontrol, privatization, and good corporate governance and market regulation. Market reform swept through the world, including countries as diverse as Argentina, Brazil, India, Mexico, New Zealand, Poland, and Russia. Most were thought to be doing virtually everything needed to spark rapid growth.

But once again the results were disappointing. By the end of the 1990s, most of these countries' growth rates had returned to levels so low that the profile of the global economic landscape wasn't changing at all. Today more than 80 percent of the world's people still get by on less than a quarter of the average income in rich countries, much as they did 50 years ago.

Even worse, only a handful of countries, having moved out of dire poverty into the middle ground, enjoy a real prospect of joining the rich ones (see "A steep climb"). This failure is worrisome because it means that today's poor countries will probably be poor 20 years from now. Economic development is a slow process. Even if poor countries grew at the extraordinary rate of 7 percent a year, it would take them 50 years to catch up. At *current* rates, it would take them a couple of centuries—if they ever did. As the tenacity of oppressive regimes and the rise in terrorism in these poor countries amply demonstrate, this gap between rich and poor is a major threat to global stability.

Conventional solutions have failed because they don't address the real causes of persistent poverty. The Washington consensus, like the 50 years of development economics before it, is

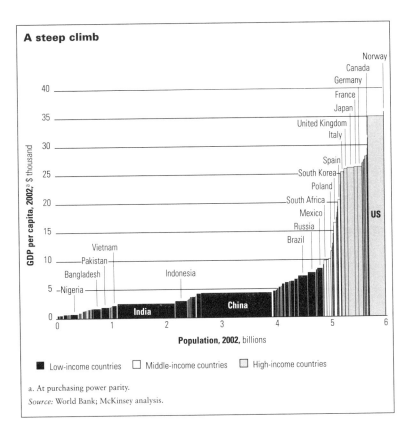

A steep climb

GDP per capita, 2002,[a] $ thousand

Population, 2002, billions

Norway
Canada
Germany
France
Japan
United Kingdom
Italy
Spain
South Korea
Poland
South Africa
Mexico
Russia
Brazil
Vietnam
Pakistan
Bangladesh
Indonesia
Nigeria
India
China
US

■ Low-income countries ☐ Middle-income countries ☐ High-income countries

a. At purchasing power parity.
Source: World Bank; McKinsey analysis.

grounded in an analysis of economies at the aggregate level. But that's like trying to learn about the physical universe by using only the telescopes of astronomy; most real understanding in physics has actually come from studying the interaction of the tiniest particles in the universe. In economics, it is necessary to understand why individual companies operate as they do, since they are the ultimate sources of growth and job creation. Most economists can't afford the time and resources needed to look, in detail, at the way an entire country's economy works. They rely instead on broad national data sets and complex econometric tools that yield qualified answers at best.

At the McKinsey Global Institute (MGI) we have had, since 1990, the luxury of studying the dynamics and evolution of a representative group of industries in 13 countries: Australia, Brazil, France, Germany, India, Japan, the Netherlands, Poland, Russia, South Korea, Sweden, the United Kingdom, and the United States. In each, we analyzed the performance of 6 to 13 industries and compared it with the performance of the same industries in a handful of other countries. Our work is thus based on detailed studies of individual businesses, from state-of-the-art auto plants to black-market street vendors. It builds an understanding of the economy from the ground up, not the top down—a grassroots rather than a bird's-eye view.

This research has produced a new and unexpected understanding of the persistence of income disparities among nations. Economic progress depends on increasing productivity, which depends on undistorted competition. When government policies limit competition, even unintentionally, more efficient companies can't replace less efficient ones. Economic growth slows and nations remain poor.

It's productivity

GDP per capita is widely regarded as the best single measure of economic well-being.[2] That measure is simply labor productivity (how many goods and services a given number of workers can produce) multiplied by the proportion of the population that works. This proportion varies around the world—though, interestingly, not by much.

Productivity, however, varies enormously and explains virtually all of the differences in GDP per capita (see "Productivity paves the way"). Thus, to understand what makes countries rich or poor, you must understand what causes productivity to be higher or lower. This understanding is best achieved by evaluating the performance of individual industries, since a country's

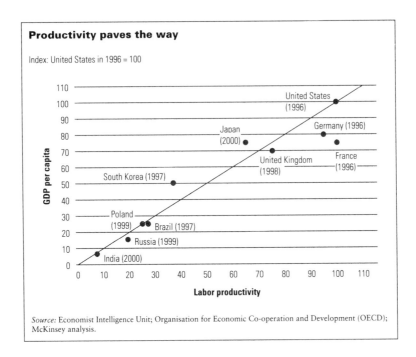

Productivity paves the way

Index: United States in 1996 = 100

Source: Economist Intelligence Unit; Organisation for Economic Co-operation and Development (OECD); McKinsey analysis.

productivity is the average of productivity in each industry, weighted by its size. Such a micro approach reveals the important fact that the productivity of industries also varies widely from country to country.

This approach yields two crucial insights. First, to understand why some countries are mired in poverty, it is necessary to look beyond broad macroeconomic policies, such as interest rates and budget deficits, and also consider the myriad zoning laws, investment regulations, tariffs, and tax codes that hold back the productivity of industries and thus a nation's prosperity. Of course, macroeconomic stability is necessary. MGI's studies of Brazil, India, and Russia show that without it companies concentrate on making money by exploiting the instability rather than by raising their productivity. Yet a stable economy alone isn't enough to make countries prosper and grow: Japan has had a stable economy for decades but has suffered from ten years of stagnation.

The second insight is the realization that the income level of a country is determined, above all, by the productivity of its largest industries. High productivity in the unglamorous "old-economy" sectors—retailing, wholesaling, construction—is most important, since more people work in them. The fabled high-tech enclaves and financial markets are less so. MGI's study of rapid US productivity growth in the 1990s found that it was caused by just six industries, including retailing and wholesaling, not by the vaunted "new economy."[3] IT investments played a modest role. In India, the fast-growing IT industry has yet to raise the living standards of more than a minuscule part of the population.

Differences in productivity also explain the persistence of disparities in wealth among rich nations. Twenty-five years ago, the economies of the United States, Europe, and Japan were generally expected to converge because technology, capital, and business practices flowed freely among them and their workforces were healthy and well-educated.

In fact, significant disparities of wealth remain even among rich countries. Despite Japan's world-class automotive and consumer electronics industries, for example, its average per capita income[4] is about 30 percent below the US average. Japan has followed a path different from that of the United States and Europe (see "The path to productivity"): economic growth during the past 30 years has been generated more by massive increases in the number of hours worked and the amount of capital equipment used than by an increase in the productivity of the

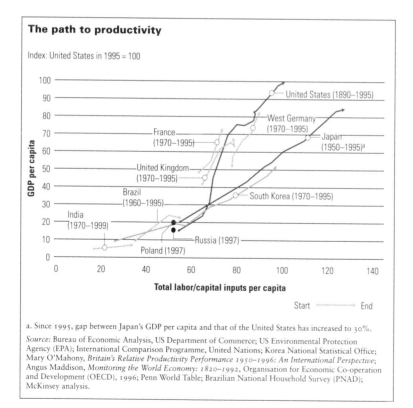

The path to productivity

Index: United States in 1995 = 100

a. Since 1995, gap between Japan's GDP per capita and that of the United States has increased to 30%.

Source: Bureau of Economic Analysis, US Department of Commerce; US Environmental Protection Agency (EPA); International Comparison Programme, United Nations; Korea National Statistical Office; Mary O'Mahony, *Britain's Relative Productivity Performance 1950–1996: An International Perspective*; Angus Maddison, *Monitoring the World Economy: 1820–1992*, Organisation for Economic Co-operation and Development (OECD), 1996; Penn World Table; Brazilian National Household Survey (PNAD); McKinsey analysis.

workforce. South Korea has followed a similar path. But there is a limit to the number of hours that can be worked, and massive inputs of capital that don't earn an economic return eventually lead to diminished growth. Since 1990, Japan's real per capita income has barely grown. South Korea's tiger economy is running out of steam as well.

Barking up the wrong tree

Many economists still attribute differences in the productivity of countries to differences in their labor and capital markets. These economists therefore believe that big investments in education and health and generous development loans and grants are the keys to economic growth. MGI's research, however, found that these factors explain few, if any, differences in economic performance.

Consider education. In the early 1990s, Germany and Japan seemed to be passing the United States in economic performance. One of the principal reasons cited was the poor education of the US workforce. Since then, Japan's carmakers have built US factories that achieve 95 percent of the productivity these companies enjoy at home. Whatever the faults of the US education system, on-the-job training clearly compensates for them.

This truth holds for poor countries as well. Some of Brazil's private retail banks are as efficient as any in the world. South Korea's POSCO (formerly Pohang Iron & Steel) may have the highest productivity of any integrated steel producer. Carrefour operates with nearly the same efficiency in emerging markets and in Europe. Poor education systems haven't hindered these companies. If illiterate Mexican immigrants can reach world-class productivity levels building apartment houses in Houston, illiterate Brazilian workers can do so in São Paulo.

Similarly, MGI found that a lack of capital to finance investment isn't the main constraint on growth in poor economies. If local businesses organized and managed themselves as the world's best companies do, they would unleash rapid productivity growth. About 20 percent of India's people work in companies that are structured somewhat like those in the developed world, but their average labor productivity is only 15 percent of what their US counterparts achieve. MGI calculated that these companies could increase their productivity to about 40 percent of the US average without any additional capital investment,[5] just by reorganizing the way they conduct work. In 1983, the high-performing Japanese auto company Suzuki Motor invested in a joint venture to make cars in India. Suzuki, which had operational control, built plants like the ones in Japan, organized the work as it is organized in Japan, and trained employees to work as they do in Japan. As a result, the productivity of these facilities is 55 percent of the US auto industry average.

Poor countries thus don't have to wait until they build bigger and better school systems and educate a whole generation of workers. Nor do they need to wait for more development aid from rich countries. If local businesses followed the proven approaches for organizing production and managing a workforce, poor countries could grow much faster than most people realize. Domestic savers and foreign investors hungry for good returns would also supply these countries with plenty of capital for new investments.

Competition is the key

If differences in labor and capital markets don't matter, what does? In each of 13 country studies, MGI found that the primary answer was the nature of competition in product markets.

Competition is the mechanism that helps more productive and efficient companies expand and take market share from less productive ones, which then go out of business or become more efficient. Either way, consumers benefit as companies offer better goods at lower prices, and this may in turn unleash a burst of new demand.

But government policies sometimes stand in the way of competition and prevent innovation from spreading. Such policies might exclude potential competitors, such as start-ups or foreign companies, or might favor particular classes of companies, such as mom-and-pop retailers. Often, policies (zoning laws, for example) have unintended consequences for business. When they do, competition is less intense and inefficient companies aren't pressured to change. Productivity growth is slower and countries remain poor.

The Washington consensus of the 1990s profoundly underestimated the importance of a level playing field for competition. Over and over again, MGI found industries in which more productive innovators were excluded and less productive companies favored. In much of Europe, for instance, zoning laws prevent large retailers from expanding as fast as they could and therefore from replacing less efficient small retailers. Because retailing is one of the largest sectors in most economies, it has important ramifications for a nation's standard of living. For instance, Tesco, the United Kingdom's largest food retailer, has failed to obtain planning permission to build a modern supermarket on the site of a derelict hospital—broken windows and all—near central London because the building is over 100 years old. The result of such failures is lower productivity for the UK economy and higher food prices for consumers.

In Japan, a combination of zoning laws, tax policies, and government subsidies has allowed the smallest, most inefficient retailers to thrive. Today they account for slightly over half of all retailing employment, compared with less than 20 percent in the United States. In one small shop in central Tokyo, I have seen the same hat sit unsold on a store shelf gathering dust for the past 15 years. Every time I'm in Tokyo, I check to see if the hat is still there. It is. The proprietors don't have to sell it to stay in business, since they get subsidized loans. Their shop sits on some of the world's most valuable land, so they know their estate will repay the loans.

Even the United States isn't immune to policies that limit competition. The 2002 steel tariffs, which have since been declared illegal by the World Trade Organization and withdrawn, protected US steel producers from lower-cost foreign competitors. The recent increase in US agricultural subsidies does the same.

Poor countries, however, have adopted much more severe market-distorting measures. After the Soviet Union's fall, a flurry of new business activity took place in Russia. It was assumed that more productive companies would replace the unproductive Soviet ones and that Russia would rapidly become rich. But MGI found that the new Russian companies were no more productive than their Soviet predecessors. Why? More productive companies either tried to enter the market and failed or didn't bother to try. For instance, Carrefour, perhaps the best international retailer, concluded that it couldn't make money in Russia. Like virtually all multinationals, Carrefour pays taxes. The competitors it would face in Russia—the open-air markets—don't and thus have a decisive tax advantage. Before the ruble crashed in 1998, open-air markets also sold smuggled or counterfeited goods at prices Carrefour couldn't match.

A similar situation exists in Brazil. About 50 percent of its workers aren't registered with the government. Although many of these people are poor and wouldn't be taxed heavily, the total revenue forgone is substantial because of the number of workers involved. As a result, Brazil must collect twice as much in profit, employment, value-added, and sales taxes from corporations as the United States does to finance its government.[6] When taxes are included, it costs more productive companies as much to do business as it costs less productive, informal ones, which don't pay taxes. Modern, productive enterprises can't easily take market share from their unproductive counterparts, and the economy's natural evolution is stymied.

Meanwhile, in India the government has directly limited competition by insisting that several hundred consumer goods can be manufactured only in small-scale plants. As a result, Indian consumers pay higher prices than they should, and India, unlike China, hasn't become a global center of low-cost manufacturing. (China actually exports to India.) Moreover, in housing construction, competition among developers and construction firms is based not on cost and productivity advantages but on gaining control of scarce parcels of land with clear ownership titles. Over 90 percent of land titles in India are subject to dispute, and nobody is going to invest in land someone else might claim.

If poor countries eliminated the policies that distort competition, they could grow rapidly. India's government, for instance, abandoned many of the limits on foreign investment in the country's automotive industry during the early 1990s. Subsequently, prices fell, demand for cars exploded, and output nearly quadrupled (see "Invisible hand, visible results").

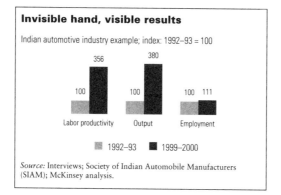

Invisible hand, visible results

Indian automotive industry example; index: 1992–93 = 100

Source: Interviews; Society of Indian Automobile Manufacturers (SIAM); McKinsey analysis.

The barriers to growth

The main obstacles to economic growth in poor countries are the many policies that distort competition. Why are they so pervasive?

For one thing, most people favor the social objectives that inspire high minimum wages, small-business subsidies, and other business policies. They may not be aware of the unintended adverse consequences that create major barriers to growth. Instead of attempting to achieve social objectives by limiting competition, countries should allow fair competition and thereby generate more national income, which can then be redistributed through taxes and government subsidies for the desperately poor.

Even more important, countries have bad policies because they benefit certain people. In rich countries, special interests generally aren't allowed to have their way so much that they can significantly undermine the common good. Most poor countries lack these limits. Moscow's government officials, for instance, allocate housing contracts to their cronies in the old Soviet construction companies. As a political favor to small companies that can't pay their bills, local governments in Russia prevent energy companies from cutting off their power. India's domestic retailers are wholly protected from foreign direct investment by global best-practice retailers.

In poor countries today, every domestic firm is a potential special interest that stands to lose from more competition. These unproductive firms' workers often think, mistakenly, that they too stand to lose. Certainly, the prospect of finding new work in an economy where most jobs pay near-subsistence wages is frightening. But to have healthy economies, countries must allow unsuccessful owners and managers to fail so that more productive ones can take their place. In that healthier economy, workers will find a better job market.

Think consumer

Undoubtedly, dismantling barriers to economic growth is difficult. Some firms must be allowed to go out of business, thus forcing workers to find new jobs. Industries must be opened to foreign competition, and the enforcement of tax codes and other regulations must be strengthened. And governments must stand up to special interests.

How can countries muster the political will to do all these things? The answer lies in focusing on consumers, not producers. Many people think that production itself creates economic value—an idea that sometimes makes governments protect businesses regardless of their performance. This approach is mistaken. Such people and governments fail to understand the link between production and consumption. Goods have value only if consumers want them. Otherwise sheer production does little to raise standards of living.

Most poor countries are far from having a consumption mindset. Their governments and leaders, like those of the former

Soviet Union, focus instead on output. A consumption mind-set requires some notion of individual rights, including the right to buy what you want from anybody who wishes to sell it to you. Consumers want to patronize companies that offer better products and services or lower prices. Those are the companies that survive if competition is equal. Thus, consumer interests are served when competition isn't distorted.

If policymakers in poor countries—and the many development experts who advise them—can accept this overlooked fact, those countries could unleash rapid growth. Only then will the shape of the global economic landscape begin to change for the better.

William W. Lewis,
McKinsey Quarterly, 2004 Number 2.

Notes

1. For more on the failure of development economics, see William Easterly, *The Elusive Quest for Growth: Economists' Adventures and Misadventures in the Tropics*, Cambridge, Massachusetts: MIT Press, 2002.

2. Some people argue that indicators of health, life expectancy, and social well-being are just as important, if not more so. But men and women the world over want more than a subsistence living, and that is why millions of them emigrate from poor countries to rich ones, even doing so illegally and risking their lives in the attempt. The Soviet Union achieved military power but ultimately collapsed because it didn't provide enough consumer goods.

3. See William W. Lewis, Vincent Palmade, Baudouin Regout, and Allen P. Webb, "What's right with the US economy," *The McKinsey Quarterly*, 2002 Number 1, pp. 30–40 (www.mckinseyquarterly.com/links/3896).

4. Measured at purchasing power parity, not current exchange rates. PPP compares standards of living in different countries more accurately because it measures the amount of goods and services different currencies can command in their home markets.

5. Because of low labor rates, the lack of automation would prevent them from matching US productivity.

6. Brazil's bloated government contributes to the high tax burden and thus is an obstacle to growth. It currently spends 39 percent of the nation's GDP, compared with 37 percent in the United States. Back in 1913, when the United States had the same per capita income Brazil has now, the US government spent only 8 percent of the country's GDP.

2

Regulation that's good for competition

Scott C. Beardsley and Diana Farrell

IDEAS IN BRIEF

Economic regulation should facilitate fair competition while mitigating the impact of market failures.

Despite good intentions, regulation often has negative consequences. Rules to guarantee good minimum wages, for instance, often limit the creation of jobs for low-skilled workers.

A fact-based approach and a transparent process are essential for optimal regulatory decisions. So is controlling special-interest groups.

Regulation should protect people rather than jobs, let the market pick winning companies and technologies, and take account of the infrastructure needs of nations—and of the differences among them.

The aim of economic regulation should be the same in all sectors: to facilitate fair competition among players or, where natural monopolies exist, to ensure fair pricing and service levels. Greater competition means stronger productivity growth, which in turn means a faster-growing economy and more wealth to share. Yet governments everywhere struggle to get regulation right.

Why regulate at all? First, market economies can't function properly without rules: property rights (including trademarks and patents that protect innovators) underpin transactions, and antitrust laws safeguard fair competition. The painful transition away from Communism in the former Soviet Union is a particularly vivid example of the need for a basic legal framework. Second, regulation is necessary to mitigate broader market failures in generally competitive industries—for example, to protect consumers from abusive practices, to introduce and maintain safety standards, to protect vulnerable workers, and to control environmental pollution. Moreover, some forms of regulation (such as orphan-drug rules for rare diseases) aim to force or encourage businesses to meet the vital needs of unprofitable customers. Third, regulatory intervention is vital in supporting competition and so promoting the welfare of consumers in their dealings with electricity, telecommunications, and other network industries that tend to monopoly because of huge infrastructure requirements.

Regulation often runs into substantial difficulties, however. For starters, there is no manual for implementing market-supporting regulations. When regulators define rules of competition in areas such as predatory pricing and intellectual property, they must constantly strike a tricky balance. Rules and standards to protect consumers must be sufficient, but not so costly as to discourage innovation and halt progress. Governments are too inclined to frame policy through trial and error, confusing economic goals with political and social ones. Although such experiments often reflect genuine choices about the type of market competition a society wishes to have, pressure from special interests for state intervention may not be benign and may completely undermine the economic rationale for regulation. Thus governments sometimes—and often unintentionally—devise rules that hamper competition and create long-term drags on growth.

The McKinsey Global Institute (MGI) believes that poor regulation is the main factor limiting productivity and growth in economies throughout the world, particularly developing ones. India, for example, could raise its labor productivity by 61 percentage points if it removed harmful rules. Brazil could raise its labor productivity by 43 percentage points (see "The regulation straitjacket"). MGI research on Russia suggests that more effective regulation in that country, principally to ensure fair competition, could raise its structural economic growth rate to as much as 8 percent a year without significant capital investment, which it now struggles to raise despite current high oil prices.

In a recent study of 145 countries, the World Bank[1] found that the administrative cost of complying with regulations is three times higher for businesses in poor countries than for those in rich ones. Yet businesses in poor countries have less than half the protection for property rights. Heavy regulation and weak property rights, moreover, exclude the poor from business. Women, young, and low-skilled workers suffer most.

Companies in both developing and developed economies are worried. A CEO survey presented at the 2005 World Economic

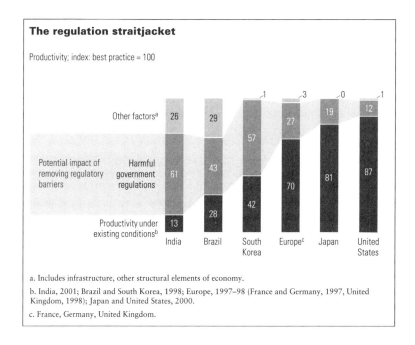

The regulation straitjacket

Productivity; index: best practice = 100

a. Includes infrastructure, other structural elements of economy.

b. India, 2001; Brazil and South Korea, 1998; Europe, 1997–98 (France and Germany, 1997, United Kingdom, 1998); Japan and United States, 2000.

c. France, Germany, United Kingdom.

Forum, in Davos, identified overregulation as the most important threat facing businesses. How can governments craft more effective and balanced regulations? MGI studies of 17 economies, as well as McKinsey's long and deep experience working with regulators and businesses, have helped us identify three common regulatory traps and some basic principles to help rule makers avoid them.

Inappropriate regulation of factors of production

Governments sometimes restrict competition in a wide range of sectors by inappropriately regulating markets for factors of production, such as labor and property. They try to prevent abuses and correct market failures, but their efforts frequently have unintended consequences.

Costly labor market regulations

Perversely, regulations that protect jobs often constrain employment. Managers who have only a limited ability to reduce the workforce in a downturn are hesitant to hire new workers. This reluctance makes it harder for competitive companies to grow.

Furthermore, regulations guaranteeing decent wages for the most poorly paid workers often limit the creation of new low-skill jobs in service industries. France, for instance, sets its minimum wage at a level twice that of the United States. As a result, US retailers employ 50 percent more people per capita than do their French counterparts. Although not plum jobs, these do boost the economy's overall ability to create wealth while helping many low-skilled employees avoid social exclusion and giving them an opportunity to move up the income ladder. Instead of raising the minimum wage, with its possibly damaging secondary effects, governments can provide assistance to low-income workers by using earned-income tax credits to reduce their taxes.

Restrictive land and property regulations

Regulating land and property can slow growth by inhibiting capital investment and industrial consolidation. Japan's zoning laws, for example, protect mom-and-pop retail shops but prevent the expansion of more productive large-scale discounters. Small shops account for more than 50 percent of the Japanese retailing sector, compared with less than a quarter in the United States.

Unclear land titles and property rights also stifle growth. In the Philippines, as Hernando de Soto shows in *The Mystery of*

Capital: Why Capitalism Triumphs in the West and Fails Every-where Else,[2] it can take 13 to 25 years and almost 170 steps and signatures to acquire a piece of land legally. As a result, 60 to 70 percent of the country's people don't have legal title to their land. This problem not only precludes the development of a mortgage market and, hence, of a robust financial system but also removes the main source of collateral for small-business owners and entrepreneurs. It is also hard for bigger companies to obtain enough land.

Overregulation of competitive sectors

In most countries that MGI has studied, the biggest constraints on economic growth result from inappropriate and unevenly enforced regulations in naturally competitive manufacturing and service sectors, such as consumer goods and construction.

Protectionist market entry regulations

To protect local industry and employment, governments create barriers such as import tariffs and restrictions on foreign direct investment. But protection of this kind insulates local companies from competition and so removes their incentive to provide better and cheaper goods and services, thereby harming the broader economy.

In India, for example, a small-scale-reservation law designates hundreds of products that only companies below a certain size may manufacture. It also restricts investments in fixed assets by companies that produce most of their output for the domestic market. Both domestic and foreign manufacturers therefore can't reach economies of scale.

Restrictive product market regulations

Governments rightly create safety standards to ensure that electrical appliances are not a fire hazard and food standards to protect the people's health. But some product market regulations make it harder for companies to innovate and become more productive. In the long run, consumers and the whole economy lose out.

Japan's regulations governing the materials and techniques used in home construction, for example, aim to preserve the national character of the country's building stock. They work: every house in Japan looks different from other houses and is uniquely Japanese. But the construction industry can't raise its productivity through standardization, which would make housing cheaper. It would be better if consumers could decide for themselves whether to pay an aesthetic premium.

Germany restricts the hours when retail stores can be open in order to protect their workers and to make Sundays special. But these regulations, combined with high minimum wages and with zoning laws limiting hypermarkets, have helped keep the productivity of German retailing 15 percent below that of retailing in the United States.

Inflexible regulation of former monopoly industries

When governments liberalize utilities, railroads, and other network industries, the potential productivity gains are enormous. Utilities usually account for 10 percent or more of a nation's GDP, and their prices affect the performance of companies throughout the economy.

To create competition in sectors such as telephony and electricity, regulators often try to lessen the market power of incumbent former monopolists. One common approach involves requiring them to let new retailers use their networks at a favorable wholesale price while still insisting that they provide universal coverage for profitable and unprofitable customers alike. Competition is vibrant in such former monopoly industries of most developed economies. The transfer of profits away from the incumbents has been substantial, and prices have tumbled in some sectors: from 1990 to 2002, for example, the cost of fixed-line telephone calls fell by almost 50 percent in the countries of the Organisation for Economic Co-operation and Development (OECD) (see "Plummeting"). The granting of licenses to a host of new mobile-telephony operators has also increased competition and demand, improved the infrastructure, and cut prices.

Governments, however, often struggle to create flexible frameworks that anticipate and respond to conditions as markets evolve. In telecommunications, for example, regulators in developed markets are struggling to take account of new technologies that, along with existing regulations, are changing the balance

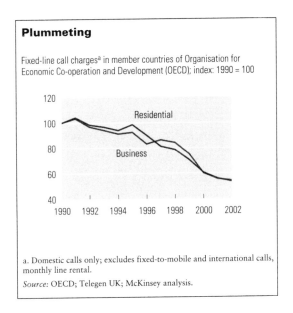

Plummeting

Fixed-line call charges[a] in member countries of Organisation for Economic Co-operation and Development (OECD); index: 1990 = 100

a. Domestic calls only; excludes fixed-to-mobile and international calls, monthly line rental.

Source: OECD; Telegen UK; McKinsey analysis.

of power between incumbents and attackers. Although alternative platforms such as cable, wireless, and VoIP (Voice over Internet Protocol) are substitutes for traditional fixed-line telephony, they tend to be regulated separately and, in some cases, circumvent regulation altogether.

As a result, the challengers are gradually eroding fixed-line telephony, which still generally accounts for a majority of the revenues and profits of the incumbents. Under current cost structures, if such regulatory asymmetries are not adjusted to reflect the new reality they will severely reduce the returns of the incumbents' fixed-line business. That will in turn undermine the incumbents' ability to invest in new infrastructures and technologies (such as a national broadband network) that would benefit consumers and the overall economy in the long term.

Getting regulation right

Regulators should keep certain guidelines in mind as they tackle the difficult task of making their rules more effective.

Make regulation fact based and transparent

A fact-based approach and a transparent process are the keys to making optimal regulatory decisions and controlling special-interest groups. Regulators should understand not only how different options will affect the economics of competition in a sector but also their social and political implications. Detailed modeling and analysis are required to clarify the trade-offs and to judge whether the goals of regulation will be met.

Some governments that formerly failed to undertake this kind of analysis are now changing their ways. Until now, for example, India's government has banned foreign direct investment in the retail sector in the belief that modern formats favor the rich and that greater competition wouldn't drive substantial growth elsewhere in the economy. But having undertaken a microeconomic analysis showing that modern-format discounters offer lower prices and that a competitive retail sector would generate productivity growth in one-third of the total economy, the government may lift the ban.

Making regulatory barriers more transparent—for example, by measuring levels of regulation against international benchmarks—helps a country develop a community of support for regulatory reform and therefore puts pressure on the special interests behind the status quo. A community of this kind often includes academics, international organizations (such as the World Bank and the Asian Development Bank), the global media, influential private foundations, private individuals, and, of course, representatives of the one group likely to benefit most: consumers.

Make regulation dynamic

Dynamic rule making is particularly important in heavily regulated sectors. A regulator should continually assess not only the kinds of rules each of them requires but also, if competition is already established, whether fewer rules might make sense. Like taxes, regulations are hard to remove or reduce, but doing so may be necessary to stimulate growth and innovation.

Regulators can make rules more malleable by adopting a "sunset" clause that requires regular reviews of how well regulations fulfill their purpose and either extends their sunset dates or automatically terminates them at a particular time. The US Civil Aeronautics Board Sunset Act of 1984, for example, ended nearly 40 years of close regulation of airline routes and fares by the CAB. This move led to intense competition and to lower prices that helped consumers and the US economy at large.

Today many regulatory laws are also subject to impact assessments: systematic examinations of the advantages and disadvantages of ways to achieve an objective. Most OECD countries have adopted this approach, but they don't use it to the same extent, and many developing countries don't use it at all. Some governments have also established independent consultative bodies, such as the United Kingdom's Better Regulation Task Force.

Regulate factor markets with care

Reforming the rules covering the factors of production can have a major impact. Because of the complex and sensitive trade-offs between economic and social objectives, however, reform must be handled with great care if it is both to win broad support and create economic value.

Spain achieved both goals in the 1990s, when it introduced more flexible labor laws that helped cut unemployment by 40 percent in only six years. Among other things, the reforms let employers and employees negotiate contracts (rather than having labor laws dictate the terms) and created a new type of permanent contract, which reduced the employers' payouts to laid-off workers by 60 percent, for youths and other groups that have unusual difficulty finding jobs.

Belgium, by contrast, maintains generous early-retirement schemes intended to promote corporate restructuring and to keep the peace with labor. But they have generated huge costs for the government and given the country one of Europe's lowest employment rates. Only one in four Belgians aged 55 to 64 works.[3]

Let the market pick the winners

Regulations governing competitive markets should be neutral in their impact on different players. Leveling the field for new entrants, whether at home or abroad, spurs competition by pressing incumbents to match or surpass their productivity. When governments take this perspective, they avoid the regulatory trap of trying to protect enterprises of every scale, from mom-and-pop stores to national airlines.

Regulators clearly have a role in developing national technological standards. But with rare exceptions, they should avoid favoring one product or technology over another, since doing so often reduces incentives to compete and innovate. Europe's decision to deploy the Global System for Mobile Communications (GSM) and to allow roaming and interoperability across borders was effective because these moves helped mobile technology to penetrate European markets more quickly than it did elsewhere. But European telecom ministries had previously urged (and sometimes forced) operators to buy telecom equipment made in the home country—a decision that drove costs much higher than they would otherwise have been.

Enforce regulations evenly

Allowing some players to gain advantage by disregarding the rules also distorts competition. When regulators fail to tackle the gray (informal) economy, in which companies underreport employment, avoid paying taxes, and ignore product quality and safety regulations, the market can't pick the winning products and services. Companies operating partially or wholly outside the law gain substantial cost advantages, which more than offset their low productivity and small scale and help them stay in business. Larger, more productive, and law-abiding companies therefore can't gain market share—a huge problem in low-income nations, where the informal economy generates an estimated 40 percent of GNP. It is widespread in some developed nations too.[4]

To address the problem, governments must devote enough resources to pay for adequate enforcement of tax and other regulations. Many developing countries in particular will have to improve their tax collection and audit capabilities and to increase penalties for those flouting the law. To avoid massive social repercussions in the transitional stage and to increase the chances of success, governments should address the informal economy one sector at a time.

Protect people, not jobs

When regulators try to save employment in a particular sector, they may succeed for a period, but at the expense of job creation elsewhere in the economy. In the United States, for example, anxiety about losing service jobs to offshore providers is widespread. But MGI research indicates that the US economy as a whole gains sizable benefits from offshoring, through corporate savings, additional exports, repatriated profits, and greater productivity.

Rather than seeking to prevent the loss of jobs eliminated through the search for higher productivity, regulators should focus on cushioning the blow for workers who become unemployed and on easing their transition to new jobs. Such assistance could include retraining programs and company-sponsored insurance to offset lower wages. From 1979 to 1999, however, 69 percent of the US workers who lost their jobs through the offshoring of services found new work within six months, and roughly half moved to higher-value-added activities.[5]

In many Western European countries, regulators should also facilitate the creation of new jobs by making labor and product market rules more flexible so that they don't stifle competition and innovation.

Don't regulate business processes

In naturally competitive and liberalized sectors, businesses should be free to decide how best to meet any standards for the health and safety of their products and for protecting the environment. If governments use restrictive regulations to control the operations, organizational structure, and practices of companies— including the way they satisfy their demand for labor—their ability to innovate in pursuit of greater productivity will suffer.

Consider the 1990 US Clean Air Act amendments, which established a "cap-and-trade" system to reduce sulfur dioxide emissions from coal-powered electricity plants. By setting a cap while giving companies the option of trading their rights, regulators encouraged utilities to explore innovative ways of reducing emissions. Companies had an incentive to cut their emissions costs to levels below the market price for the rights and to sell their excess rights to other companies. The scheme achieved its targets more cheaply than expected: experts predicted that the cost of reducing sulfur dioxide emissions would range from $700 to $1,500 a ton, but the final market price of the rights reflected a cost of only $350.

Tailor regulation to national markets

Regulation must reflect the legal and institutional background of specific countries as well as their stage of economic and infrastructure development; copying foreign regulations is rarely appropriate and can be downright harmful. Although benchmarks help to increase transparency, they must be comparable. Factors such as the cost of capital, labor rates, population density, demand patterns, the competitiveness of the industrial structure, and the stage of liberalization vary widely by country. Benchmarks should thus be tailored to the local environment, since they can drive very different regulatory outcomes.

Many developed economies that moved quickly to privatize telecommunications were acting logically when they based their regulatory regimes on the role of the fixed-line incumbents that then dominated the industry. But in some developing countries (including the Czech Republic, Jordan, Malaysia, and Russia), the incumbents' fixed-line networks already have far fewer users than new mobile networks do. In such cases, mobile may be a much more efficient way to provide universal service. It might be appropriate to regulate both kinds of networks in a similar way to ensure the widespread development of a mobile data infrastructure at generally accessible prices.

Remember the need for infrastructure

Rail and telecom networks, water and gas pipelines, and distribution grids are all capital intensive, with long payback periods. Regulators should consider ways to promote and reward investment in these networks. One way might be to let prices for network access be higher than its actual cost so that incumbents can reinvest in or upgrade networks and new players find it worth-while to build their own. Another possibility is "ring-fencing" new investments by, say, guaranteeing that a new telephony net-work investment won't be available to other players for a period of time.

Make natural-monopoly trade-offs explicit

Clearly, some cases will involve natural monopolies (or tem-porary ones in industries such as pharmaceuticals) as well as many types of rail and power infrastructures. Here regulators should make explicit trade-offs between the tight regulation of pricing and the interests of consumers, on the one hand, and the effects of regulation on employment, investments in infrastructures, business models, innovation, quality, universal service, and the like—elements that competition usually drives—on the other. Rural mail, telephony, and rail service, as well as the pricing of orphan drugs for rare diseases, are just a few such questions. The key is to analyze facts and objectives so that their implica-tions become clear and to make explicit trade-offs among the interests of diverse groups of stakeholders. Issues such as cross-subsidies, the protection of intellectual property, and predatory pricing must constantly be evaluated and addressed in these kinds of environments.

Crafting regulations that encourage rather than hinder competi-tion and growth is increasingly tough at a time of accelerating technological change and economic uncertainty. Politicians are under pressure to protect troubled industries and to safeguard jobs. The work of regulators is ever more complex—which makes it ever more vital that they make wise choices.

Scott C. Beardsley and Diana Farrell,
McKinsey Quarterly, 2005 Number 2.

Notes

1. International Finance Corporation and World Bank, *Doing Business in 2005: Removing Obstacles to Growth,* Oxford University Press, September 2005; and World Bank, *World Development Report 2005: A Better Investment Climate for Everyone,* Oxford University Press, September 2004.

2. New York: Basic Books, 2000.

3. *Prospero: A New Momentum to Economic Prosperity in Belgium* (2004) is available at www.mckinsey.com/locations/benelux/work/prospero/index.asp. The work is based on data from established Belgian sources, such as the Federal Planning Bureau, the National Bank of Belgium, and the National Institute of Statistics; from international organizations, including the OECD; and from discussions with union leaders, politicians, academics, and top executives at Belgium's private and public institutions.

4. Diana Farrell, "The hidden dangers of the informal economy," *The McKinsey Quarterly,* 2004 Number 3, pp. 26–37 (www.mckinseyquarterly.com/links/17280).

5. Lori G. Kletzer, *Job Loss from Imports: Measuring the Costs,* Institute for International Economics, Washington, DC, September 2001 (www.iie.com).

3

What's right with the US economy

William W. Lewis, Vincent Palmade,
Baudouin Regout, and Allen P. Webb

IDEAS IN BRIEF

The primary source of productivity gains from 1995 to 1999 was not the stock market bubble, or information technology. Instead, the gains were caused by managerial and technological innovations in six sectors: wholesale, retail, securities, semiconductors, computer manufacturing, and telecommunications.

The relationship between IT and labor productivity is extremely variable. In rare cases, IT can deliver extraordinary productivity improvements. More often, creative managers use IT to redesign core business processes, products, or services.

The important questions for longer term are: whether the acceleration of productivity from 1995 to 1999 is sustainable and what the behavior of the rest of the economy will be.

As companies attempt to cope with an economic downturn and the United States fights a war on terrorism, many wonder whether the long-term health of the US economy will be undermined. The answer depends on what happens to the productivity growth rate—the main determinant of how fast the economy can grow. At issue is whether the near doubling of US productivity growth rates during the late 1990s, from 1.4 percent (1972–1995) to 2.5 percent (1995–2000), can continue.

Our yearlong research[1] indicates that many of the product, service, and process innovations underlying the productivity acceleration of the late 1990s will continue to generate productivity growth rates above the 1972–1995 trend for the next several years, although probably not as high as those of 1995 to 1999. Higher productivity, in turn, will boost economic growth.

Surprisingly, the primary source of the productivity gains of 1995 to 1999 was not increased demand resulting from the stock market bubble, as some economists have claimed. Nor was information technology the source, though companies accelerated the pace of their IT investments during those years.[2] Rather, managerial and technological innovations in only six highly competitive industries—wholesale trade, retail trade, securities, semiconductors, computer manufacturing, and telecommunications—were the most important causes (see "Six sectors led the way").[3] The other 70 percent of the economy contributed a mix of small productivity gains and losses that offset each other. In addition, cyclical demand factors were important in some parts of the economy.

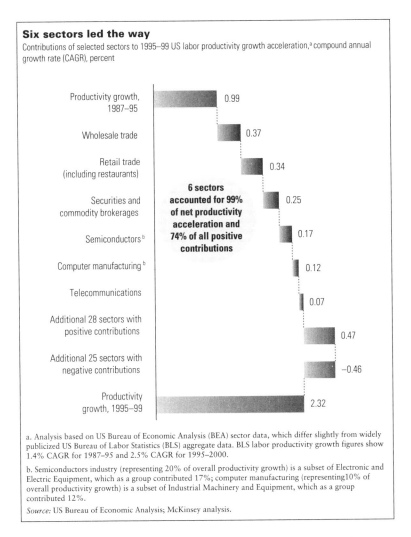

Six sectors led the way

Contributions of selected sectors to 1995–99 US labor productivity growth acceleration,[a] compound annual growth rate (CAGR), percent

Productivity growth, 1987–95	0.99
Wholesale trade	0.37
Retail trade (including restaurants)	0.34
Securities and commodity brokerages	0.25
Semiconductors[b]	0.17
Computer manufacturing[b]	0.12
Telecommunications	0.07
Additional 28 sectors with positive contributions	0.47
Additional 25 sectors with negative contributions	−0.46
Productivity growth, 1995–99	2.32

6 sectors accounted for 99% of net productivity acceleration and 74% of all positive contributions

a. Analysis based on US Bureau of Economic Analysis (BEA) sector data, which differ slightly from widely publicized US Bureau of Labor Statistics (BLS) aggregate data. BLS labor productivity growth figures show 1.4% CAGR for 1987–95 and 2.5% CAGR for 1995–2000.

b. Semiconductors industry (representing 20% of overall productivity growth) is a subset of Electronic and Electric Equipment, which as a group contributed 17%; computer manufacturing (representing 10% of overall productivity growth) is a subset of Industrial Machinery and Equipment, which as a group contributed 12%.

Source: US Bureau of Economic Analysis; McKinsey analysis.

It is not unusual, we found, for only a small number of sectors to experience a productivity jump during any four-year period. But in the late 1990s, these six sectors, departing from the norm, either enjoyed extremely large leaps in productivity (for instance, semiconductors and computer manufacturing) or accounted for a large share of employment (retail and wholesale).

At the national level, the relationship between IT spending and productivity is unclear. Many sectors other than the six jumping ones increased their pace of IT investment but experienced stag-nant or even *slower* productivity growth (see "It takes more than just IT"). We found an inconclusive correlation between the acceleration of IT investments and changes in productivity growth. In fact, taken as a group, the other 53 economic sectors had almost no productivity growth.

The challenge, then, was to understand what caused the pro-ductivity acceleration in the six key sectors. We did a detailed study of these sectors, as well as three others that invested heav-ily in IT but failed to boost productivity—hotels, long-distance data telephony, and retail banking.

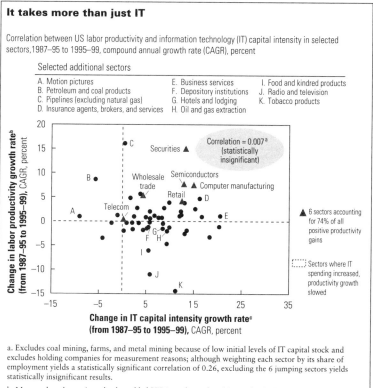

It takes more than just IT

Correlation between US labor productivity and information technology (IT) capital intensity in selected sectors,1987–95 to 1995–99, compound annual growth rate (CAGR), percent

Selected additional sectors

A. Motion pictures
B. Petroleum and coal products
C. Pipelines (excluding natural gas)
D. Insurance agents, brokers, and services

E. Business services
F. Depository institutions
G. Hotels and lodging
H. Oil and gas extraction

I. Food and kindred products
J. Radio and television
K. Tobacco products

a. Excludes coal mining, farms, and metal mining because of low initial levels of IT capital stock and excludes holding companies for measurement reasons; although weighting each sector by its share of employment yields a statistically significant correlation of 0.26, excluding the 6 jumping sectors yields statistically insignificant results.

b. Measured as change in real value added PEP (people employed in production).

c. Measured as change in real IT capital stock PEP.

Source: US Bureau of Economic Analysis; McKinsey analysis.

Explaining the 1995 productivity acceleration

Within the six jumping sectors, the most important cause of the productivity acceleration after 1995 was fundamental changes in the way companies deliver products and services. Sometimes these innovations were aided by technology (whether new or old), sometimes not. In all six sectors, high or increasing competitive intensity was essential to the spread of innovation, and in two sectors, regulatory changes played an important role in raising that intensity. Cyclical demand factors and a shift in consumer purchasing patterns toward higher-value goods were important in explaining the acceleration of productivity in retail, wholesale, and securities.

Structural factors: Competition and innovation

The bulk of the acceleration in productivity after 1995 can be traced to managerial and technological innovations that improved the basic operations of companies. These innovations were structural and are likely to persist. Sometimes, the catalyst was a dominant player with a superior business model; other times, it was managers using new technology to redesign core operations.

In general-merchandise retailing, productivity growth more than tripled after 1995 because competitors started more rapidly adopting Wal-Mart's innovations—including the large-scale ("big-box") format, "everyday low prices," economies of scale in warehouse logistics and purchasing, and electronic data interchange (EDI) with suppliers. As a result, Wal-Mart's competitors increased their productivity by 28 percent from 1995 to 1999, while Wal-Mart itself raised the bar further by increasing its own productivity by an additional 22 percent. Although e-commerce grew rapidly during this period, its penetration (0.9 percent of retail sales in 2000) was too low to make a difference in overall retail productivity. We estimate that Internet commerce contributed less than 0.01 percentage points to the 1.33 percent jump in economy-wide productivity growth.

The operations of wholesalers underwent similarly dramatic changes during the middle of the 1990s as new warehouse-management systems were adopted (see "The changing warehouse"). Pharmaceuticals wholesalers, for instance, responded to increasing price pressure from large retailers by automating distribution centers. Because each center keeps an inventory of tens of thousands of different items, stocking, picking, and shipping have traditionally been highly labor-intensive. The combination of pre-1995 hardware (bar codes, scanners, picking machines) and software for tracking and controlling inventory allowed wholesalers to automate their flow of goods partially and to increase their labor productivity greatly.

In computer manufacturing, nearly all of the productivity

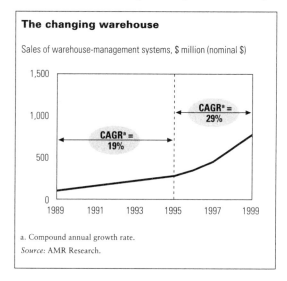

The changing warehouse

Sales of warehouse-management systems, $ million (nominal $)

CAGR[a] = 29%

CAGR[a] = 19%

a. Compound annual growth rate.
Source: AMR Research.

acceleration was due to innovations outside the sector itself. Technological improvements in microprocessors and other components (memory, storage devices), as well as the integration of new components (CD-ROMs, DVDs), caused an acceleration in the value of computers produced. At the same time, the popularization of the Internet and the accelerating processing requirements of Microsoft's Windows operating systems (see "A decade of speedier PCs") caused a spike in demand for more powerful personal computers. These two factors further contributed to the high productivity growth in the manufacture of computers and semiconductors.

Productivity growth in the semiconductor industry accelerated mainly because the performance of the average chip did. Largely in response to competitive pressure from Advanced Micro Devices, Intel took less time to bring out new and better chips than it had done previously.

The securities industry was the only sector we studied in

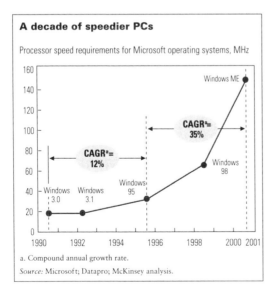

A decade of speedier PCs

Processor speed requirements for Microsoft operating systems, MHz

a. Compound annual growth rate.

Source: Microsoft; Datapro; McKinsey analysis.

which the Internet materially boosted productivity. At the end of 1999, roughly 40 percent of retail securities trades were being conducted on-line, up from virtually zero in 1995, and a given number of frontline employees can now broker ten times as many trades as they could then. Competition from on-line discount brokers, such as E*Trade and Charles Schwab, was critical to the rapid diffusion of these innovations in the traditional brokerage houses.

Regulatory changes increased competition and had a significant effect on productivity in some cases. In the securities industry, the US Securities and Exchange Commission's order-handling and 16th rules[4] sharply reduced transaction costs, allowing institutional investors to take advantage of increasingly small price anomalies and boosting trading volumes. In the telecom sector, the licensing of new spectrum for mobile telephony heightened competition and sparked faster price decreases, lifting both penetration and usage. In both the securities industry and the telecom sector, larger volumes allowed industry players to leverage fixed costs.

Cyclical demand factors

Some of the acceleration in productivity after 1995 was due to demand factors that may not be sustainable. In the securities industry, the soaring stock market led to productivity advances in three different ways (see "Cyclical demand in the securities industry"). First, lofty index values (particularly Nasdaq's) fueled a surge in on-line retail trading. Second, they also increased the value of assets under management, boosting the productivity of money managers. Finally, they increased the number and value

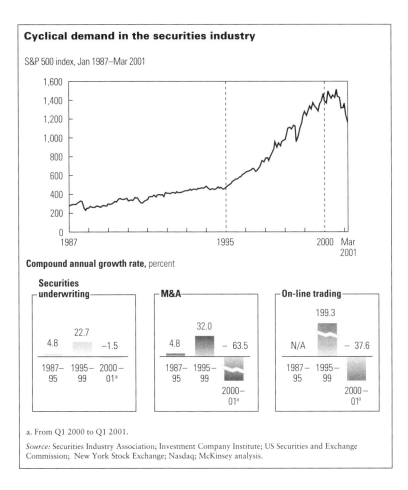

Cyclical demand in the securities industry

S&P 500 index, Jan 1987–Mar 2001

Compound annual growth rate, percent

Securities underwriting

4.8   22.7   −1.5

1987– 95   1995– 99   2000– 01[a]

M&A

4.8   32.0   − 63.5

1987– 95   1995– 99   2000– 01[a]

On-line trading

N/A   199.3   − 37.6

1987– 95   1995– 99   2000– 01[a]

a. From Q1 2000 to Q1 2001.

Source: Securities Industry Association; Investment Company Institute; US Securities and Exchange Commission; New York Stock Exchange; Nasdaq; McKinsey analysis.

of initial public offerings and of mergers. These factors explain half of the productivity jump observed in the securities industry.

In general-merchandise retailing, and most likely in the rest of retail and in wholesale, almost half of the measurable productivity jump reflected the higher value of the goods that consumers increasingly favored. Retailing experts believe that the shift was mainly the result of growing confidence, income, and wealth rather than a marked improvement in the retailers' techniques of enticement.

The role of information technology

Contrary to conventional wisdom, the widespread adoption of information and communications technology was not the most important cause of the acceleration in productivity after 1995. Our nine sector case studies clearly show that the relationship between IT and labor productivity is extremely variable.

In rare cases, IT can deliver truly extraordinary productivity improvements, expanding labor capacity by an order of magnitude. As mentioned above, on-line securities trading requires only a fraction of the frontline labor employed in traditional channels. In mobile telecommunications, cellular equipment employing new digital standards made better use of the available spectrum, spurring rapid price declines and a spike in usage. In both cases, the product or service itself, being intangible information that could easily be digitized, was highly susceptible to such improvements.

In most cases, however, IT was just one of many tools that creative managers used to redesign core business processes, products, or services. A significant portion of Wal-Mart's business innovations (such as the big-box format) was independent of IT. Where IT did play a role, it was a necessary but not a sufficient enabler of productivity gains. To reap the full productivity benefits of inventory-management systems or EDI, for instance, a business must implement operational-process changes. The same is true of the automation of warehouse and distribution centers in the wholesale sector.

To understand why IT is not a panacea, we looked at three sectors that invested heavily in IT but experienced no improvement in productivity growth: hotels, the long-distance data portion of the telecom sector, and retail banking. Some spending on

IT in these sectors and elsewhere in the economy was designed to maintain capabilities, such as investments in Y2K compliance and more rapid upgrades of personal computers to ensure compatibility with emerging Windows standards. Other IT expenditures, on things such as Internet and corporate-networking equipment, were made to generate future rather than immediate productivity benefits. The confluence of these unusual demand factors explains most of the acceleration in IT spending from 1995 to 1999.

It is also possible that IT increases the consumer's convenience in ways that are not fully captured by government productivity measures. Even so, this would not be sufficient to explain the "IT paradox." Hotels invested heavily in creating central reservation systems that provided customers with some unquantifiable value (for instance, immediate, centralized information on the availability of rooms), but the increase in convenience was probably modest. The added convenience of on-line banking also doesn't appear in government productivity measures. But even if it were possible to correct for this measurement problem, the small number of on-line transactions would not have been enough to reverse the deceleration of productivity growth in retail banking.

Some IT investments do not appear to be delivering the intended results, and whether they ever will remains to be seen. Retail banks and hotels, for instance, have collected significant amounts of customer data that they have yet to use productively. Companies in the retail-banking industry bought an average of two PCs per employee from 1995 to 1999. Some of this computing power was not fully utilized and some, it is likely, never will be.[5] Long-distance telephone players made enormous investments in metropolitan and long-haul networks that are currently underutilized and will probably remain so for several years to come.

Our conclusion about the effect of IT on productivity is straightforward. IT can be quite valuable when deployed as part of a management plan to reorganize specific core activities of a business. In this respect, it is not different from other forms of capital—new building designs, new materials-handling systems, new semiconductor production tools. But when generic IT solutions are applied to support functions, or when IT represents no more than a "me-too" investment, it is unlikely to move the needle on a company's productivity. A robust explanation of the recent acceleration in productivity must therefore go well beyond IT.

The future of US productivity

An important question for the longer term is whether the acceleration in productivity from 1995 to 1999 is sustainable. We estimate that at least half of what occurred in the six jumping sectors can be sustained over the next five years. Wal-Mart still enjoys a sizable productivity advantage over its competitors and will continue to force efficiency improvements in the industry. The limited penetration of warehouse automation (now at just 25 percent), and, to a lesser degree, of mobile telephony and online trading, leaves room for further growth, and thus productivity gains, in those sectors. Both the computer-manufacturing and semiconductor industries should benefit from a continuation of the current rate of improvement in the performance of microprocessors.

Clearly, however, some of this acceleration will be unsustainable. The burst in demand for personal computers is behind us, and the effects of the stock market bubble on asset valuations, M&A, and securities trading have already largely evaporated. We

cannot judge whether consumers will continue to shift their purchasing patterns in favor of higher-value goods at the 1995–1999
rate or know what will happen in the portions of the retail and
wholesale sectors that we did not study.

A larger source of uncertainty about future productivity growth
is the behavior of the rest of the economy. A review of the performance of the other 53 sectors over the past two decades reveals
that both their contribution to national productivity growth and
their average annual productivity growth rate have been quite
small. Those figures, however, show considerable volatility—
some of it caused by business cycles and some by changes in industry dynamics and structure. If historical precedents hold, this
kind of noncyclical volatility could reduce the national rate of
productivity growth over the next four years by 0.1 percentage
points annually or increase it by as much as 0.4 percentage points
annually.

It is possible that other sectors of the economy will defy the
historical trend and experience extraordinary productivity jumps.
The key contributor to such jumps would be innovations, such
as Wal-Mart's improvements in its business system or on-line
securities-trading technology, that streamlined labor-intensive activities or leveraged fixed labor costs. Competition, which could
be triggered by regulatory changes, is required to diffuse innovation. A quick scan of the economy revealed several sectors showing
the first signs of emerging innovators (such as software; media,
including motion pictures; insurance carriers; and depository
and nondepository institutions) and of promising regulatory
changes (electric, gas, and sanitary services as well as pharmaceuticals). However, the number of these sectors, their share of
total employment, and the potential magnitude of their jumps

are not impressive. Therefore, we believe, continuing volatility in the rest of the economy's productivity growth rate is likely to encompass the effect of these innovations and regulatory changes.

Although uncertainty about the performance of all these factors makes precise predictions impossible, our analysis indicates that overall productivity growth could be as low as 1.6 percent or as high as 2.5 percent.[6]

Even our low estimate offers ample reason for optimism about the US economy, regardless of what happens in the short term. The six key sectors will continue to generate above-trend productivity growth for at least several more years. No one can predict when and where the next entrepreneurial initiative will strike outside of these sectors. But healthy levels of competition, 20 years of deregulation, and a long tradition of US ingenuity will allow the country's economy to continue to define the productivity frontier.

US productivity after the dot-com bust

Diana Farrell, Martin Baily, Jaana Remes

In the second half of the 1990s, US labor productivity surged. It grew at 2.5 percent a year, up from an annual average of just 1.4 percent between 1972 and 1995. But then the dot-com bubble burst. Many observers expected productivity growth to fizzle out too, as companies reined in spending and struggled against the economic downturn. But productivity continued to grow at an impressive 2.6 percent a year to the end of 2003, the most recent date for which government figures on productivity by sector are available.

The report predicted that the product, service, and process innovations underlying the productivity performance of the six key sectors could sustain growth of at least half the 1995–2000 rate over the next five years, in the range of 1.6 to 2.4 percent. In fact, productivity growth stayed near the top of the range. But did the contributions by sector change?

Changes in the way industry data are compiled mean it is not possible to make comparisons over a long period. However, consistently compiled data from 1998 to 2003 allow for some useful comparisons (see "1998–2000: four sectors led the way" and "2000–2003: more evenly distributed productivity growth"). Over those five years, only a few sectors were responsible for most of the productivity growth, just as we found in our earlier research. Seven sectors accounted for 85 percent of total productivity growth over the period, five of them broadly similar to key sectors identified in our previous study: wholesale trade, retail trade, finance and insurance, computer and electronic products, and broadcasting and telecommunications.[a] These sectors had a disproportionate effect on the direction and rate of productivity change nationally either because they were such large employers or because they grew so rapidly. However, productivity growth since 2000 is somewhat less concentrated among the big hitters than before: between 1998 and 2000, the top four sectors represented 100 percent of total growth; from 2000 to 2003, the top seven sectors contributed only 75 percent of the total.

Since 2000, some of the sectors with the fastest growing productivity in 2000 saw growth slow down substantially—notably computers (although this comes as no surprise given the passing of Y2K and the dot-com bust). Yet the productivity growth rates in retail and wholesale trade have continued to accelerate from their already rapid rate. And interestingly, a much broader set of service industries have also seen their productivity growth speed up, including administrative support and scientific and technical services, as well as construction and restaurants. As a result, five of the top contributors to productivity acceleration after 2000 were service industries. Given that services represent 70 percent of US employment today, this is very good news indeed.

One reason that productivity growth held up so well from 2000 to 2003 is that fewer sectors than in our previous study saw their productivity decline, possibly the result of successful efforts by companies to cut costs. Sector productivity data beyond 2003 is not yet available, but recent figures for overall US productivity growth show that, while it has come down from its 2003 peak, it is maintaining a respectable 2.3 percent. This should be seen as a normal correction rather than a return to the listless productivity growth of 1972 to 1995. Indeed, the data from 2000 to 2003 shows plenty of scope remaining for most sectors to produce more for less. As long as competition between companies remains intense, the United States can look forward to strong productivity growth in the years to come, with all that implies for improvements in living standards.

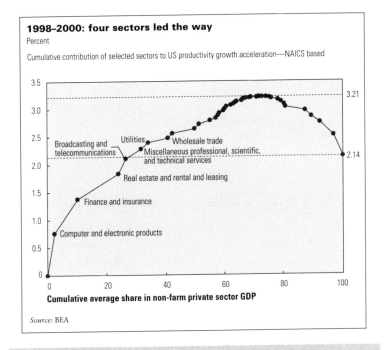

1998–2000: four sectors led the way

Percent

Cumulative contribution of selected sectors to US productivity growth acceleration—NAICS based

Source: BEA

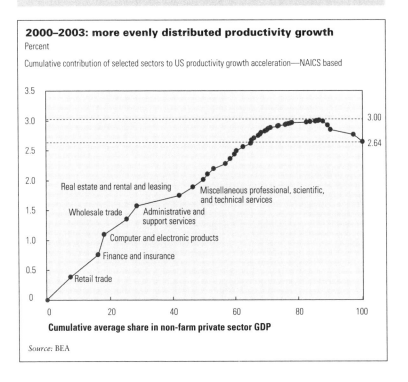

2000–2003: more evenly distributed productivity growth
Percent

Cumulative contribution of selected sectors to US productivity growth acceleration—NAICS based

Source: BEA

---

[a]Real estate is a newcomer, but productivity in that sector wasn't measured under the old scheme, partly because it is so hard to capture.

William W. Lewis, Vincent Palmade, Baudouin Regout, and Allen P. Webb, *McKinsey Quarterly,* 2002 Number 1.

Notes

1. The study on which this article is based involved a collaboration of the McKinsey Global Institute, the Firm's high-technology practice, and the San Francisco office. Greg Hughes, James Manyika, Lenny Mendonca, and Mike Nevens helped lead the project. The research team, which deserves special recognition, included Angelique Augereau, Mike Cho, Brad Johnson, Brent Neiman, Gabriela Olazabal, Matt Sandler, Sandra Schrauf, Kevin Stange, Andrew Tilton, and Eric Xin. The full study is available on-line at www.mckinsey.com/mgi.

2. Between 1987 and 1995, information technology investments by US companies rose by a compound annual rate of 11 percent. Between 1995 and 1999, this compound annual growth rate jumped to 20.2 percent.

3. These six sectors accounted for virtually all of the net productivity acceleration and for 74 percent of all positive contributions.

4. The 16th Rule refers to the SEC's 1997 mandate to quote securities prices in increments of 1/16th rather than 1/8th. The New York Stock Exchange and the Nasdaq started experimenting with decimalization even before the SEC's April 2001 deadline.

5. From 1995 to 1999, banks spent a total of $5,253 per employee (in nominal dollars) on new PCs.

6. For a full explanation, see chapter 3 of the full report, at www.mckinsey.com/mgi.

4

Reviving French and German productivity

Diana Farrell, Heino Fassbender, Thomas Kneip, Stephan Kriesel, and Eric Labaye

IDEAS IN BRIEF

Differences in IT spending are not the root cause of the gap between US and European productivity. Europe's basic problem is inappropriate regulation that hinders innovation.

A part of the lagging productivity growth in France and Germany is explained by the nature of their consumer demand as compared to that of the United States, and by their lower income per head.

The need to increase productivity in Germany and France is driven by the coming aging workforce and demographic shift.

F or most of the second half of the 20th century, France and Germany progressively narrowed their labor productivity gap with the United States. That changed in the 1990s, however, as US productivity growth pushed ahead and growth in Europe slowed. By 2000, its labor productivity gap with the United States had widened again, to 5 percent for France and to 15 percent for Germany (see "The gap widens").[1]

One cause is clear: both France and Germany have smaller IT-manufacturing sectors than does the United States, where IT generates 2.3 percent of GDP. US productivity in this sector—which benefited from more powerful and easily assembled computers, from advances in microchips, and from a spike in demand—rose

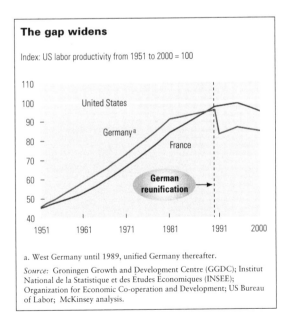

The gap widens

Index: US labor productivity from 1951 to 2000 = 100

a. West Germany until 1989, unified Germany thereafter.

Source: Groningen Growth and Development Centre (GGDC); Institut National de la Statistique et des Études Économiques (INSEE); Organization for Economic Co-operation and Development; US Bureau of Labor; McKinsey analysis.

sharply in the late 1990s. Indeed, studies show that the sector accounted for about a quarter of the annual US productivity growth during this period. Meanwhile, in France and Germany, where IT manufacturing generated only 1.3 and 1.5 percent of GDP, respectively, the sector contributed less than a fifth of total productivity growth. But this difference explains only a third of the gap in productivity growth between the two European countries and the United States since the mid-1990s.

Many observers blame the remaining gap on the lower levels of IT spending in Europe. In aggregate, French and German companies do spend less on technology than US companies do (see "France and Germany spend less on IT"), but low IT investment isn't the root cause of lower productivity growth; it is necessary to ask *why* companies in the two European nations invest less in technology. Besides, spending money on IT doesn't guarantee higher productivity.[2] IT *can* play a valuable role in developing innovative products, services, and processes that raise productivity, especially if deployed in highly consolidated sectors or in transactions involving high volumes per customer, so that the benefits can be spread across a larger customer or sales base. But IT spending can also yield disappointing results—as

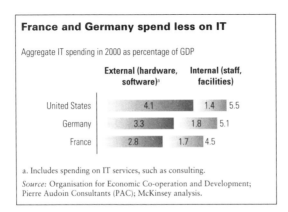

France and Germany spend less on IT

Aggregate IT spending in 2000 as percentage of GDP

	External (hardware, software)[a]	Internal (staff, facilities)	
United States	4.1	1.4	5.5
Germany	3.3	1.8	5.1
France	2.8	1.7	4.5

a. Includes spending on IT services, such as consulting.

Source: Organisation for Economic Co-operation and Development; Pierre Audoin Consultants (PAC); McKinsey analysis.

many retail banks found after investing in customer-relationship-management (CRM) systems.

It is only through an examination of productivity at the sector level that the true drivers of, and barriers to, productivity growth emerge. In 2002, the McKinsey Global Institute (MGI) compared six sectors—automotive, retail banking, retail trade, road freight, telecommunications, and utilities—in France, Germany, and the United States to see how the two European countries could increase their rate of productivity growth.[3] The analysis provided a mixed picture (see "Productivity performance at the sector and subsector levels"). While productivity had grown strongly in almost all sectors studied, the details were starkly different. In

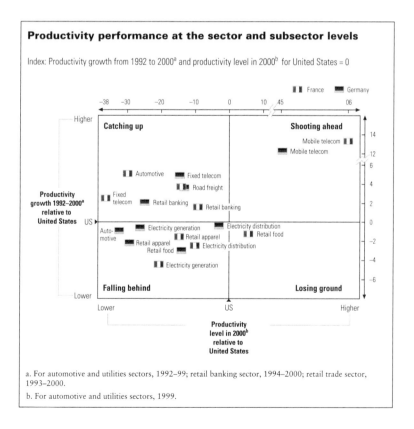

Productivity performance at the sector and subsector levels

Index: Productivity growth from 1992 to 2000[a] and productivity level in 2000[b] for United States = 0

a. For automotive and utilities sectors, 1992–99; retail banking sector, 1994–2000; retail trade sector, 1993–2000.

b. For automotive and utilities sectors, 1999.

most sectors in France and Germany, productivity was 10 percent or more behind US levels. Some European sectors, such as retail banking, continue to close the gap; others, such as retail trade, are falling further behind. In the mobile-telecom industry, productivity levels and growth rates are much higher in France and Germany than in the United States.

What accounts for these disparities? The sector studies underpin our belief that differences in IT spending have not been the cause of the differences between the productivity of the United States and that of France and Germany. Rather, it is inappropriate regulations that distort the competitive environment and stifle innovation in the two European countries. The adoption of innovative products, services, and processes—which may or may not involve the use of IT—has played a critical role in raising productivity in France and Germany as well as in the United States. Although consolidation too plays a part, in the longer term the only sustainable source of rising productivity is innovation. That means new products and services, such as mobile telephony, which gave rise to a fast-growing new business, and new (and often IT-enabled) processes, such as back-office automation, which allowed financial institutions to process a high volume of transactions with little added cost for each one.

Blame inappropriate regulation

Innovations can be expensive and may require changes in the way managers run their businesses. Without intense pressure from competitors that exploit best-practice processes, managers thus often shy away from adopting them. Zoning laws, for example, protect French food shops, whether hypermarkets or small traditional providers, from new competition. By slowing down growth in the number of retail-food outlets, these regulations have lifted capacity utilization, thereby raising productivity to levels higher than those prevailing in Germany or the United States. However, in this environment, French food retailers, including the large operators, have been slow to adopt best-practice innovations, such as collaborative supplier relationships that create greater efficiencies by reducing inventories and keeping shelves stocked with popular items. Productivity growth in the retail-food sector is now slower in France than in the United States, and without a more rapid adoption of best-practice innovations the French advantage in this subsector will slip away.

Conversely, France's automotive sector demonstrates how deregulation and competitive pressure can spur innovation and raise productivity. The Japanese first introduced lean manufacturing—aimed at eliminating waste and reducing assembly time—in the automobile industry during the 1970s. But in France, as elsewhere, tariffs protected national carmakers from cheaper imports. Shielded against competition, French companies maintained the operational status quo. In the 1990s, trade barriers gradually fell at a time when the Western European car market was stagnating. French carmakers found themselves losing market share. In response, they moved to adopt industry best practices, including lean manufacturing, which made labor productivity rise more rapidly in the French sector than in its German counterpart and narrowed the productivity gap between French carmakers and US and Japanese ones (see "France narrows the automotive gap"). The partial privatization of Renault and management changes there and at PSA Peugeot Citroën were also important milestones in promoting the adoption of lean-manufacturing techniques.

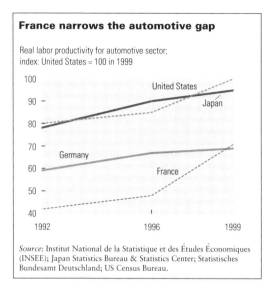

France narrows the automotive gap

Real labor productivity for automotive sector;
index: United States = 100 in 1999

Source: Institut National de la Statistique et des Études Économiques
(INSEE); Japan Statistics Bureau & Statistics Center; Statistisches
Bundesamt Deutschland; US Census Bureau.

A lack of competitive pressure to adopt best practices quickly
wasn't the only problem. The others included inappropriate regulations as well as ownership structures that support fragmented
markets and hinder consolidation, for scale plays a significant
role in increasing productivity by spreading fixed costs, including fixed labor, across a broader customer base and by helping
companies take full advantage of innovation and thereby encouraging further improvements in productivity. But in Germany,
small state-owned and cooperative retail banks, for example,
are ubiquitous, and since their owners are not answerable to the
capital markets, they have little incentive to consolidate. The
country's banking sector pays a heavy price in productivity for
this fragmentation (see "A high level of fragmentation retards
productivity in German banking").

By contrast, the deregulation of the European road freight industry sparked a wave of consolidation, and French and German
trucking companies have profited from the resulting increase in

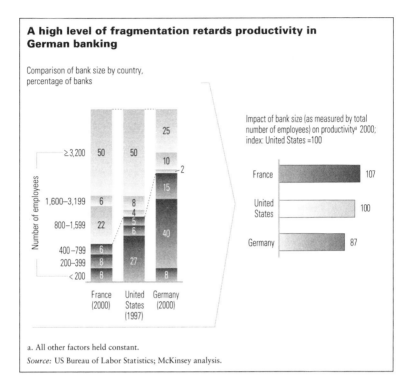

A high level of fragmentation retards productivity in German banking

Comparison of bank size by country, percentage of banks

Impact of bank size (as measured by total number of employees) on productivity[a] 2000; index: United States =100

a. All other factors held constant.

Source: US Bureau of Labor Statistics; McKinsey analysis.

capacity utilization and productivity. These networks are now large enough to let French and German road freight companies efficiently deploy tools, such as route optimization systems, that further raise their productivity. Using such tools would have made little sense for small operators.

Productivity disadvantages caused by distorted patterns of competition put a heavy burden on governments to continue and even accelerate the trend toward deregulation, though in sectors such as utilities and telecommunications, where heavy fixed costs naturally limit competition, it will be necessary to craft smart regulations that create dynamic incentives to improve productivity.[4] In our study, we found many examples of companies that enjoyed higher productivity growth in the aftermath of regulatory changes, but in many sectors there is still room for further change to promote consolidation and the more rapid dispersal of innovation. When the competitive environment is right, businesses in France and Germany will not only quickly adopt innovations that promote productivity but also invest in the IT systems that will enable or enhance them.

Demand differences also shape productivity

A part of the lagging productivity growth of the two European countries is explained by the nature of their consumer demand as compared with that of the United States and by their lower income per head. Like the scale effects resulting from consolidation, greater aggregate demand improves the utilization of fixed assets. Demand for higher-quality goods can raise productivity as well, since consumers usually pay premium prices for branded or luxury products.[5]

Differences in demand can reflect structural factors such as climate and geography as well as individual preferences. US households, for instance, spend twice as much time on long-distance calls over fixed-line networks as do French households, though prices are similar in both countries. The fixed-line grid in the United States thus has much higher utilization and productivity. In networked sectors such as utilities, telecom, and banks, with their branches and ATMs, productivity is especially vulnerable to low utilization resulting from low demand.

Varying income levels can also affect demand, since relatively prosperous people tend to buy more (and higher-quality) goods and services than do relatively poor ones. Average annual incomes in both France and Germany are 30 percent lower than those in the United States. The difference is the result of lagging productivity in Europe and lower labor inputs in Germany and

France: a smaller proportion of the working-age population labors for fewer hours a week in France and Germany than in the United States, partly because workers in Europe prefer longer vacations, shorter work weeks, and earlier retirement to higher income.

Previous MGI studies have shown that labor market rigidities too are a significant factor in Europe's lower labor inputs. The higher minimum wage in France and Germany,[6] for example, raises unemployment and keeps down the number of jobs for low-skilled workers and, consequently, income per head.

The automotive sector gives a clear example of how demand affects productivity. In recent years, US demand for SUVs and other light trucks has boomed, and they now account for more than half of the vehicles sold in the United States. These light trucks are easy to make and deliver 30 percent more value per hour worked. By contrast, in France and Germany there is more demand for small, fuel-efficient cars, which generate lower value added per hour worked. In this sector, the nature of demand in the two European markets explains a third of their productivity gap with the United States.

Europe's aging population brings urgency

The need to increase productivity in Germany and France goes beyond any theoretical race with the United States. France and Germany—indeed, all Europe—lie on the brink of a demographic shift: in a few decades, the population will have aged considerably, putting a much larger burden on the workforce. Today, for example, Germany has 2.3 people of working age for every pensioner, but by 2030 that ratio will have shrunk to 1.4. The working population will therefore be forced to support a larger group of pensioners. Short of the unexpected—increased immigration or longer working hours—the only way to maintain or improve today's standard of living in France and Germany will be to push forward productivity improvements as quickly as possible. Both countries could in fact do so.

Diana Farrell, Heino Fassbender, Thomas Kneip,
Stephan Kriesel, and Eric Labaye,
McKinsey Quarterly, 2003 Number 1.

Notes

1. To measure national labor productivity, we compared GDP to total hours worked and then adjusted the result to exclude the public sector (because its output is almost impossible to measure) and to account for the lower minimum wage in the United States. The wage effect was eliminated to create comparable working groups. About 10 percent of the US workforce consists of low-productivity workers who earn less than the effective minimum compensation levels in France and Germany.

2. See William W. Lewis, Vincent Palmade, Baudouin Regout, and Allen P. Webb, "What's right with the US economy," *The McKinsey Quarterly*, 2002 Number 1, pp. 30–51 (www.mckinseyquarterly.com/links/3896).

3. The study on which this article is based involved a collaboration between the McKinsey Global Institute and McKinsey's French and German offices. The international team was led by Thomas Kneip and Stephan Kriesel and assisted by the members of the economic advisory board: Martin Baily, of the Institute for International Economics, in Washington, DC; Olivier Blanchard, of the Massachusetts Institute of Technology; Hans Gersbach, of the University of Heidelberg; Monika Schnitzer, of the University of Munich; Nobel economics laureate Robert Solow; and Jean Tirole, of the University of Toulouse. The full study is available on-line at www.mckinsey.com/knowledge/mgi.

4. One example of smart regulation can be found in the UK utilities sector, where the authorities have imposed price caps that decrease with time. This approach pressures network operators to improve their productivity or face decline.

5. Since the value added per hour of labor is usually higher for premium goods and services, productivity rises as more of them are produced and sold.

6. Although Germany has no single minimum wage, the combined effect of wage floors set by collective bargaining and social benefits for the long-term unemployed creates what is for all intents and purposes a minimum employment cost.

5

Sweden's golden opportunity

Kalle Bengtsson, Claes Ekström, and Martin Hjerpe

IDEAS IN BRIEF

Sweden's economic revival is explained largely by the private sector's strong productivity growth, driven mostly by deregulation and intensified competition.

But productivity growth in the public sector must rise, and Sweden must improve its very poor record of creating new jobs.

These shortcomings have to be tackled as jobs migrate offshore and Sweden's population grows older. Both of these developments will put the country's large public sector under severe strain.

Swedish policymakers, companies, and trade unions must collaborate not only to remove barriers to competition in the private sector but also to improve the public sector's productivity and to create new jobs.

The economy of Sweden has made a powerful comeback after decades of steady decline, when it slipped from the ranks of the world's most prosperous nations. Since 1995, the year McKinsey last reported[1] on the country's economic performance, GDP growth has averaged 2.7 percent a year, which is stronger than that of most comparable EU countries. Per capita GDP has risen to 112 percent of the OECD[2] average, from 104 percent—a notable contrast with the continuing stagnation in Germany, France, and Italy (see "Reclaiming lost ground").

Yet any sense of satisfaction for a job well done must be tempered by an acknowledgement of the difficulties that Sweden faces as it looks ahead. Its population is aging; job creation remains anemic; and the public sector—one of the world's largest—shows few signs of the productivity growth that has revitalized the country's private-sector corporations.

Further market reforms are necessary. If Sweden is to generate sustained economic growth and to preserve the social safety nets its people hold dear, it must find ways to increase productivity in the public sector. The country must also lower the economy's total cost of labor, which currently holds back demand and thus the number of jobs created there. What's more, it must increase the flexibility of its workforce to hasten the pace of structural change in the economy, to raise the present low level of entrepreneurship, and to generate positive effects from the inevitable off-shoring of jobs over the next decade. Unless Sweden can create new ones more dynamically to replace those that go abroad, off-shoring's net effect for the country will remain negative.

Reclaiming lost ground

Top 20 OECD[a] countries by per-capita GDP; index: average for OECD[a] member countries = 100

	1970		1980		1990		1998		2004	
1	Switzerland	175	Switzerland	153	Luxembourg	150	Luxembourg	174	Luxembourg	217
2	United States	139	United States	136	Switzerland	144	United States	139	Norway	147
3	Denmark	127	Iceland	127	United States	137	Switzerland	127	United States	143
4	Luxembourg	127	Canada	123	Iceland	120	Norway	121	Ireland	131
5	Sweden	124	Luxembourg	121	Canada	115	Iceland	116	Switzerland	125
6	Canada	119	Denmark	117	Austria	114	Austria	113	Netherlands	119
7	Australia	118	Austria	115	Japan	112	Denmark	113	Austria	117
8	Netherlands	116	Sweden	115	Sweden	111	Canada	111	Iceland	117
9	New Zealand	114	Netherlands	112	Denmark	110	Netherlands	109	Australia	117
10	France	107	Belgium	111	Finland	108	Japan	108	Denmark	117
11	Germany	105	Australia	110	Germany	107	Australia	106	Canada	115
12	Austria	104	France	108	Belgium	108	Ireland	106	Belgium	113
13	Belgium	103	Germany	108	Norway	107	Germany	105	Sweden	112
14	United Kingdom	101	Norway	107	Netherlands	107	France	105	United Kingdom	111
15	Iceland	97	Italy	104	France	104	Belgium	105	Finland	108
16	Italy	97	Finland	104	Italy	104	Sweden	104	Japan	107
17	Finland	95	Japan	100	Australia	100	Italy	103	France	105
18	Japan	92	New Zealand	96	United Kingdom	98	Finland	103	Germany	104
19	Norway	89	United Kingdom	95	New Zealand	84	United Kingdom	103	Italy	99
20	Spain	76	Greece	81	Spain	80	Spain, New Zealand	82	Spain	94

a. OECD = Organisation for Economic Co-operation and Development; at current prices for given year; adjusted for purchasing-power parity.

Source: OECD annual national accounts; McKinsey analysis.

Fortunately, conditions in Sweden are favorable for such reforms. It has many productive industries—some of them world class—as well as macroeconomic stability and relatively good relations among politicians, companies, and unions. It will need to make the most of these advantages.

Looking back: Productivity turned the tide

Our 1995 study of the Swedish economy showed that both low levels of competitive intensity in a range of industries and comprehensive regulation of product markets were hobbling productivity and job creation in Sweden's industries. In a number of them, productivity was more than 20 percent lower than it was in the top-ranking countries. The result: lower growth in the economy as a whole.

From 1992 to 2004, however, overall productivity in Sweden rose by 2.4 percent a year, in line with the OECD average. Disaggregating the two components of GDP growth—productivity growth (changes in the value of output per hour worked) and adjustments in labor inputs (changes in the total number of hours worked)—makes it clear that Sweden's recovery has come about overwhelmingly through a strong increase in the productivity of the private sector, which employs about 70 percent of the workforce. Private-sector productivity has risen by 3.3 percent a year, the fourth strongest private-sector growth rate in the OECD and 1.5 times higher than the average.

At the sector level, automotive manufacturing, retailing, retail banking, and food processing have all raised their productivity substantially, both absolutely and in comparison with the same sectors elsewhere. In 1995, for instance, the Swedish retailing sector's productivity was 16 percent lower than that of the leading country, and productivity was 20 percent lower in retail banking and 42 percent lower in processed food. Since then, however, productivity has increased more quickly in each of these four Swedish sectors than in those of any of our study's benchmark countries—by 8 percent a year in automotive manufacturing, 4.6 percent in retailing and retail banking, and 3.1 percent in food processing.

The sole sector we studied that failed to improve was construction, where productivity has been growing by just 0.7 percent a year. Other countries too had low growth rates in the sector, but in Sweden it had a particularly poor starting point: in 1995, it was 25 percent less productive than its US counterpart, and its relative position has barely improved since then.

Crucial market reforms

Clearly, the reason for the productivity gains (outside of construction) is that Sweden has embraced market reforms over the past 10 to 15 years. After a deep economic crisis in the early 1990s, it gradually restored its public finances (partly by implementing a cap on spending) and introduced a restrictive monetary policy. These measures created macroeconomic stability, which has been the bedrock of the economy's development ever since. At the same time, extensive deregulation and regulatory reform, both in the country as a whole and in its individual sectors, have intensified competition within each industry and strongly lifted productivity in the private sector in general—a result that is consistent with the McKinsey Global Institute's studies of economies around the world.[3]

Three changes have been critical. The first was Sweden's entry into the European Union, in 1995. The consequent lowering of trade barriers increased competition from abroad, prompting Swedish companies to boost their efficiency. Imports of processed food, for example, increased by 8 percent a year from 1993 to

2002, prodding Swedish food processors to respond: food exports from Sweden rose by 15 percent a year over the same period. Second, stricter laws promoted fair competition. Earlier legislation along these lines had been fairly toothless; for instance, it allowed whole industries to adopt common pricing, a practice that is no longer permitted. Third, significant deregulation and regulatory reform have taken place at the sector level. Changes in zoning laws, for example, introduced greater competition in the retailing sector: since 1992, local policymakers have had to consider the positive effect of competition when would-be new entrants submit applications for retail licenses. Deregulation in retail banking too has helped new entrants obtain licenses, with the result that competition has become more intense.

The automotive sector provides a good example of how the absence of regulatory product market barriers can stimulate efficiency. Swedish automakers, with no barriers to protect them from fierce overseas competition, have constantly been forced to improve their productivity. Sweden's truck-manufacturing industry, for instance, was already the most productive in the benchmark countries when we studied it in 1995. By 2003, the overall automotive industry (trucks and cars) ranked as the world's most productive, boasted the highest level of productivity growth, and was creating the largest number of new jobs (see "In the fast lane").

One explanation for these ongoing advances is the entry of Japanese automakers into the premium segment, where Swedish-made cars compete, and the increased competitive pressure they brought. Another key factor was the cooperation and mutual understanding between Swedish employers and labor unions. Both have recognized that constant improvement is necessary for survival, so efforts to enhance production methods have been much more effective than they were in, for example, construction.

In the fast lane

Employment and productivity change in automotive industry

Net job creation, total employment in sector as % of population aged 15–64

0.15

0.10

0.05

0

−0.5

−5

0

5

10

15

Productivity change, CAGR,[c] 1992–2003, %

Germany

United States

Ireland

Netherlands

France

United Kingdom

Japan[b]

Sweden[a]

% of value added, 2003
(current prices)

3.0%
1.0%
0.1%

Productivity, 2003; index:
Sweden = 100

Sweden	100
Japan[b]	100
United States	95
France	61
Germany	59

a. Net job creation data, 1993 to 2003.

b. Net job creation data, 1992–2002; productivity data, 2002.

c. Compound annual growth rate.

Source: Groningen 60-Industry Database, Groningen Growth & Development Centre, Oct 2005; McKinsey analysis.

Sweden's construction sector shows how inappropriate regulation holds back productivity. In fact, it was the only one of the five sectors we analyzed that has remained comprehensively regulated, with few changes to its rules during the period covered by our study. Rigid zoning laws, a bureaucratic planning process, and overly detailed building codes continue to limit innovation and to make the industry inefficient. The sector's productivity hasn't improved significantly in recent years, and employment has been falling (see "Low employment for Swedish builders")—a fact of great importance because the construction industry employs 3.5 percent of Sweden's labor force and generates 4.4 percent of the GDP.[4] Inefficiencies in construction also have ripple effects in downstream industries by raising the cost of offices, factories, and housing.

Weaker public-sector productivity

The discrepancy between Sweden's annual private-sector productivity growth—3.3 percent—and the 2.4 percent increase in overall productivity during the past decade is due to the country's large public sector, which employs some 30 percent of the workforce (compared, for instance, with 10 percent in Germany). Exact productivity numbers for the public sector aren't available, partly because quantifying its many outputs (such as national defense, environmental protection, health care, and education) is hard. Nonetheless, it is clear that the public sector's productivity—like that of the rest of the economy—is closely linked to the prevailing degree of competitive intensity and to the regulatory framework.[5] Since government services in Sweden face little competition and are heavily regulated, it is reasonable to assume that productivity has improved much more slowly there than in the

Low employment for Swedish builders

Employment and productivity change in construction industry

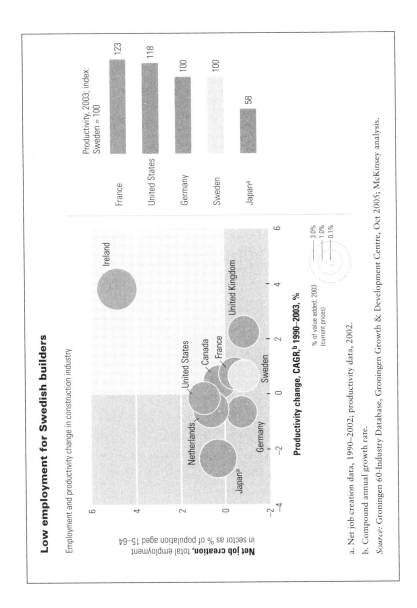

Net job creation, total employment in sector as % of population aged 15–64

Productivity change, CAGR,[b] 1990–2003, %

% of value added, 2003
(current prices)

3.0%
1.0%
0.1%

Productivity, 2003; index:
Sweden = 100

France	123
United States	118
Germany	100
Sweden	100
Japan[a]	58

a. Net job creation data, 1990–2002; productivity data, 2002.
b. Compound annual growth rate.

Source: Groningen 60-Industry Database, Groningen Growth & Development Centre, Oct 2005; McKinsey analysis.

private sector. Attempts to measure Sweden's public-sector productivity in the 1980s and early 1990s support this assumption.

A failure to create new jobs

Despite recent strong growth, Sweden's economy is still significantly weaker than others in creating new jobs. From 1992 to 2003, employment among people of working age actually *declined* by 0.4 percent a year; employment in France, Norway, and the United Kingdom, for instance, increased by 0.5 percent annually during the same period. Had Sweden, with its nine million people, achieved the same growth rate, it would have created 400,000 to 500,000 new jobs.

Sweden's failure in this respect is most apparent in the private service sector, where the country had the poorest record of the 11 we chose for comparison. From 1992 to 2003, its private service sector created a number of new jobs equal to only 4 percent of the size of the working-age population, compared with 6.9 percent in Finland, 9.2 percent in France, and 13.5 percent in the Netherlands. Sweden's relative weakness has added to the country's high real unemployment rate, which now stands at more than 15 percent; the official rate is only 5 percent, but counting all those who want to work or could do so adds at least 10 percent (see "Hidden unemployment in Sweden"). This failing is especially significant given the long-term trend, in all industrialized countries, for employment to shift from manufacturing to services.

Labor market barriers are the main reason for the private service sector's failure to create new jobs. High taxes on employment raise the cost of labor for all employers and make low-value-added services—undertaken, for instance, by restaurants, retailers, cleaning firms, and builders—very expensive. To give an example, a consumer earning a salary moderately higher than

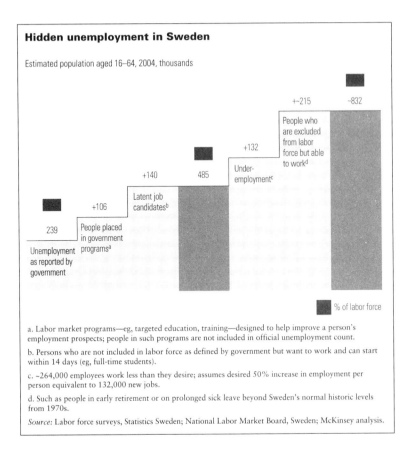

Hidden unemployment in Sweden

Estimated population aged 16–64, 2004, thousands

+~215   ~832

People who
are excluded
from labor
+132   force but able
to work[d]

Under-
employment[c]

+140   485

Latent job
candidates[b]

+106

239   People placed
in government
programs[a]

Unemployment
as reported by
government

■ % of labor force

a. Labor market programs—eg, targeted education, training—designed to help improve a person's
employment prospects; people in such programs are not included in official unemployment count.

b. Persons who are not included in labor force as defined by government but want to work and can start
within 14 days (eg, full-time students).

c. ~264,000 employees work less than they desire; assumes desired 50% increase in employment per
person equivalent to 132,000 new jobs.

d. Such as people in early retirement or on prolonged sick leave beyond Sweden's normal historic levels
from 1970s.

Source: Labor force surveys, Statistics Sweden; National Labor Market Board, Sweden; McKinsey analysis.

that of a home decorator would have to work for three or four
hours to buy one hour of the latter's time. Not surprisingly,
many Swedes choose to serve themselves as much as possible or
purchase services on the "gray" market. It is illustrative that
low-service furniture and fashion retail chains are among Sweden's most successful global companies and that Swedes spend
less of their disposable income at restaurants than do the inhabi-
tants of any other OECD country.

In addition, sector-specific regulations limit the creation of new
jobs in a number of business segments. In retailing, for example,
high statutory overtime payments make it much more expensive
than it is elsewhere for stores to stay open at the times most

convenient for customers. (Costs for retail labor rise by 70 percent on late weekday evenings and by 100 percent on weekends.) These increases curtail open hours, thereby reducing both the level of service provided to consumers and retail employment. Overall employment in retailing is much lower than it is in the United Kingdom, for example, where retail overtime rates are lower.

Rigid labor market regulations reduce productivity in construction as well, and that drives up costs and lowers demand, thus restraining employment. Surveys show, for instance, that the industry's complex piecework system for calculating wages drives up labor costs without increasing efficiency.

Laws intended to protect employees also obstruct the creation of new jobs by slowing down structural change in the economy. For example, Sweden's "last in, first out" rule—which forces public- and private-sector employers to dismiss the most recently hired workers when cutting staff—makes Swedes reluctant to move to new jobs, even at more productive companies with better growth prospects.

Challenges ahead

Sweden cannot rely on strong productivity growth in the private sector alone to drive economic growth, for three reasons. First, the improvements made since the early 1990s have been generated largely by deregulation, which enabled several sectors to catch up with and sometimes overtake their more productive foreign counterparts. However, the catch-up effect of these reforms will drop over time.

Second, demographic change will put Sweden's public sector under intolerable pressure unless its productivity improves. An aging population will require more welfare services—paid for by taxes levied on working-age people, whose share of the population is falling—and technical developments in health care constantly increase the demand for it. If nothing else changes, the resulting increase in welfare costs would become too large to finance through the current tax system in only 10 to 20 years. Even our base-case scenario indicates that the municipal income tax rate would rise to roughly 50 percent over the coming 20 to 30 years, from about 30 percent today, unless productivity rises. Since the taxpayers are hardly likely to accept such an increase, the quality of public welfare and health care services would have to decline.

Third, Sweden's real unemployment rate—15 percent—is not only serious in itself but also even more troubling in the light of accelerating globalization. As it becomes increasingly feasible to produce goods and provide services in lower-cost countries and Swedish companies feel more pressure to raise their productivity, we believe that they will move 100,000 to 200,000 jobs offshore in the next ten years. That prospect makes it imperative for Sweden's economy to become more dynamic and to create new jobs replacing those that go abroad. If the country stagnates, the cost benefits of offshoring will accrue only to companies that move jobs abroad—not to the economy as a whole.

At present, Sweden's low rate of reemployment means that the economy is a net loser each time a service job moves abroad. In contrast, the US economy derives a net gain—and improves its overall prosperity—largely because it reemploys displaced workers much more quickly. Denmark also manages to reemploy displaced workers faster than Sweden does and is consequently very close to the break-even point in the offshoring of service jobs.

Sweden must reform now

Sweden must move quickly to introduce reforms that would create favorable conditions for sustained productivity growth in the private sector, better performance in the public sector, and the creation of jobs in the private service sector.

The country's policymakers need to stimulate competition in the private sector by further deregulating the economy and adopting EU standards. In the poorly performing construction industry, for instance, Sweden should simplify its zoning laws, adopt common EU standards for materials, and reduce the sector's sizable informal component, which distorts competition by allowing certain companies to evade taxes and regulations. Moreover, the Swedish Competition Authority, which enforces antitrust laws and proposes regulatory changes to enhance competition, must continue its present work and possibly expand it. In particular, the agency should focus on the structure of many industries, including the value chains in dairy and meat production, construction materials, and food distribution, where oligopolies restrain competition.

Sweden's politicians should learn from the private sector's experience by creating similar mechanisms to improve the public sector's productivity, which must be measured to formulate growth targets and to track performance against them. Managerial responsibility for meeting these targets must be established at all levels of the public sector and competition within it intensified. One way of doing so—in education and health care, for instance—would be to let more private schools and hospitals compete with government-run institutions for publicly financed pupils and patients. Another would be to make it easier for patients to receive treatment in any public hospital they choose.

The politicians must also find ways to cut labor's total cost, which limits demand and thereby the number of jobs created in Sweden. An obvious way would be to lower Sweden's tax wedges[6] on labor, which at 44 percent rank among the world's highest. To limit the effects on public finance, such reforms might focus on private service sectors with the highest potential demand for labor.

Moreover, policymakers should consider ways of tackling the Swedish labor market's relative inflexibility, which not only limits the pace of structural change in the economy but also contributes to low levels of entrepreneurship. Neighboring Denmark's "flexicurity" model has demonstrated that it is possible to combine Anglo-Saxon labor market flexibility with Scandinavian-style unemployment benefits and active support for the efforts of the unemployed to find new jobs. Denmark's labor rules offer much less job protection than do their Swedish counterparts, but Denmark provides generous unemployment benefits and spends even more on training and other measures to improve each jobless person's employment prospects. The result has been a level of labor market turnover that is significantly higher than Sweden's.

Policymakers can't achieve the necessary outcomes on their own. Given the challenges the Swedish economy faces, politicians, companies, and labor unions must all communicate the need for reform to their respective constituencies and collaborate with each other to make reform work. The experience of Sweden's automotive industry shows that effective change comes about when all three parties understand what they must do to push ahead.

Sweden's economy has reached a critical juncture. If nothing is done, the problems will become much more serious. Quick and successful action, by contrast, would significantly increase the country's prosperity. If the private sector's productivity continues to improve at a rate one percentage point above the OECD average and the economy creates 500,000 new jobs, in ten years' time Sweden could regain the fifth place in the OECD's welfare ranking,[7] which it held in 1970.

Based on "Sweden's Economic Performance:
Recent Development, Current Priorities,"
The McKinsey Global Institute, May 2006.

Notes

1. "Sweden's Economic Performance," McKinsey Global Institute, September 1995 (www.mckinsey.com/mgi/publications).

2. The Organisation for Economic Co-operation and Development.

3. See, for instance, Diana Farrell, "The real new economy," *Harvard Business Review*, October 2003, Volume 81, Number 10, pp. 104–12; and Martin Neil Baily and Diana Farrell, "A road map for European economic reform," *The McKinsey Quarterly*, September 2005 (www.mckinseyquarterly.com/links/22141).

4. The data for the construction industry are limited to the building sector and do not include infrastructure development.

5. Thomas Dohrmann and Lenny T. Mendonca, "Boosting government productivity," *The McKinsey Quarterly*, 2004 Number 4, pp. 88–103 (www.mckinseyquarterly.com/links/22142).

6. The difference between the total labor compensation paid by an employer and an employee's take-home pay as a ratio of total labor compensation. It includes an employer's and employee's social-security contributions but not the value-added tax.

7. The OECD's ranking of member countries in terms of GDP per capita.

6

Turkey's quest for stable growth

Didem Dincer Baser, Diana Farrell, and David E. Meen

IDEAS IN BRIEF

Turkey has come a long way, but the informal economy, macroeconomic and political instability, and state ownership continue to hold it back.

Turkish productivity, now at 40 percent of the US level, could reach 70 percent if economic sectors increase productivity to their full potential.

Turkey began taking serious steps to liberalize and strengthen its economy a full 20 years ago. Before this reform program was instituted, tariff barriers were high, state ownership prevailed in key sectors, and competition was strangled by regulation. Today Turkey has plenty of modern, high-performing companies that hold their own against international competition. Many foreign companies, attracted by a relatively cheap but well-educated and skilled workforce, proximity to important markets, and the absence of major regulatory barriers, have also performed well there. So great has the country's economic progress been that it now has its sights set on becoming a member of the European Union (EU). If Turkey succeeds in its ambition, it is, based on current demographic projections, destined to be the bloc's largest member[1] and the only one with a predominantly Muslim population.

One barrier to EU accession may be Turkey's failure to achieve stable economic growth. During the 1980s, GDP grew strongly, at an average rate of 5.2 percent a year, thanks principally to the new wave of liberalization and increased competition. However, in the following decade growth fell to an average of 3.4 percent a year—lower than it was before liberalization began. Turkey's economy was battered repeatedly during the 1990s, by the Persian Gulf War of 1991, currency crises in 1994 and 1997, a devastating earthquake in 1999, and a near economic meltdown in 2001 (when GDP contracted by almost 10 percent). Some of these developments were clearly beyond the control of any government.

Yet a study by the McKinsey Global Institute (MGI)[2] suggests that the state *can* do a good deal to build the foundation of strong, sustainable economic expansion. In Turkey, as elsewhere, GDP growth depends heavily on the rate of productivity increase, and our study of 11 sectors of the economy shows that it is performing at only a little more than half of its potential productivity level.[3] To put the facts another way, Turkish productivity currently stands at just 40 percent of the US level, but we believe that it could reach 70 percent (see "The possible dream").[4]

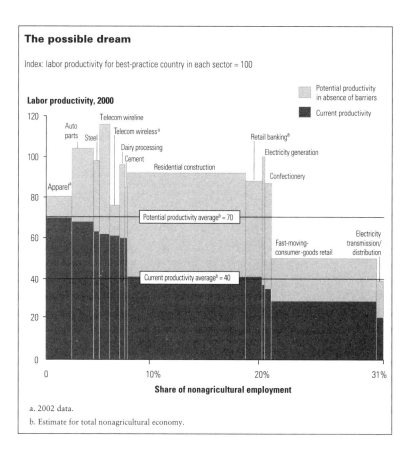

The possible dream

Index: labor productivity for best-practice country in each sector = 100

Potential productivity in absence of barriers

Current productivity

Labor productivity, 2000

a. 2002 data.
b. Estimate for total nonagricultural economy.

If Turkey took measures to realize its full productivity potential, it could create six million additional jobs by 2015 and achieve annual GDP growth as high as 8.5 percent. This would greatly improve the living standards of Turkey's 67 million people, with GDP per capita rising from around 30 percent of today's average EU per capita income (adjusted by purchasing power parity) to around 55 percent. Such convergence would substantially improve Turkey's chances for EU membership.

Compared with many other developing countries, which face dozens of barriers to productivity, Turkey is in a promising position. Thanks to economic reforms set in motion in the 1980s and to a customs union agreement with the EU in the mid-1990s,[5] many barriers to productivity evident in other countries we have studied don't exist in Turkey. It has relatively few specific product market regulations, such as pricing or product content laws, that stifle competition. We found little evidence that Turkey's labor market is handicapped by regulations, infrastructure, corporate-governance provisions, or the education of the labor force. Turkey's level of foreign direct investment is lower than that in many other developing markets but not, we believe, because of regulatory barriers (see box, "Foreign investment: A poor record," at the end of the article).

Turkey's productivity suffers from three specific problems: a large informal economy, macroeconomic and political instability, and government ownership. Together, we estimate, the three problems account for 93 percent of the gap between Turkey's current and potential productivity (see "Three fixable problems"). These are major issues, and tackling them will take sustained resolve, but at least Turkey has the comparative luxury of being able to focus on a limited number of areas for reform, and the fruits of doing so are potentially substantial.

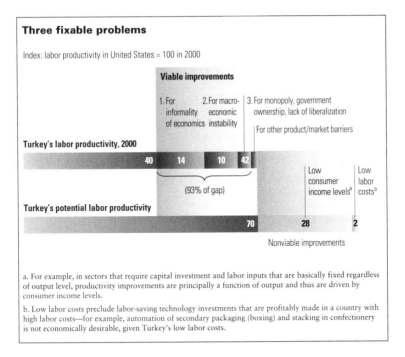

Three fixable problems

Index: labor productivity in United States = 100 in 2000

a. For example, in sectors that require capital investment and labor inputs that are basically fixed regardless of output level, productivity improvements are principally a function of output and thus are driven by consumer income levels.

b. Low labor costs preclude labor-saving technology investments that are profitably made in a country with high labor costs—for example, automation of secondary packaging (boxing) and stacking in confectionery is not economically desirable, given Turkey's low labor costs.

A two-track economy

Before analyzing the root causes of Turkey's low average productivity levels and what should be done to tackle them, it's important to recognize that this is a sharply divided economy.

In every sector, modern companies have adopted cutting-edge technologies, developed many best-practice operations, and managed to attain real economies of scale. Overall, the average productivity of such modern companies is 62 percent of the US level. However, alongside these effective performers, Turkey has many traditional entities that drag down its overall productivity.[6] They employ half of the labor force in the sectors we studied, and their average productivity is less than a quarter that of the average US enterprise. Traditional companies are typically small or midsize and tend to make relatively poor use of available technologies. Their products and services tend to be of low quality, they have few standardized production processes, and most are hampered by a lack of economies of scale.

The traditional operators' importance to the economy varies. In automotive parts, for example, they represent only 31 percent of all employment, so their drag on the productivity of the sector isn't massive; indeed, the sector's preponderance of efficient companies demonstrates how competitive intensity drives productivity. But in the retailing of fast-moving consumer goods, traditional firms account for 88 percent of all labor. Although this sector's modern players achieve 75 percent of the US productivity level, the average of the sector as a whole is therefore only 29 percent. In telecommunications, electricity generation, and retail banking—all with high capital requirements—traditional operators aren't present at all. "The curse of tradition" shows the extent to which traditional companies drag down productivity in sectors they dominate.

Clearly, the traditional companies have ample room to improve. We estimate that their doing so would close half of the gap between the country's current and potential productivity.[7] But the problems are hardly confined to traditional operators. Modern companies also underperform, for three main reasons.

First, weak organization of business processes is common. Tackling this problem offers the biggest opportunity to improve productivity. Many retailers of fast-moving consumer goods, for example, don't have sophisticated logistics-management systems, so sales losses are high. In banking, lengthy credit checks are the norm even when they are clearly unnecessary. And government-owned monopolies—particularly the electricity and wireline telephone businesses—are overstaffed. Almost half of the employees in the electricity industry aren't needed. Second, low capacity utilization, due to overestimates of demand and to a lack of com-

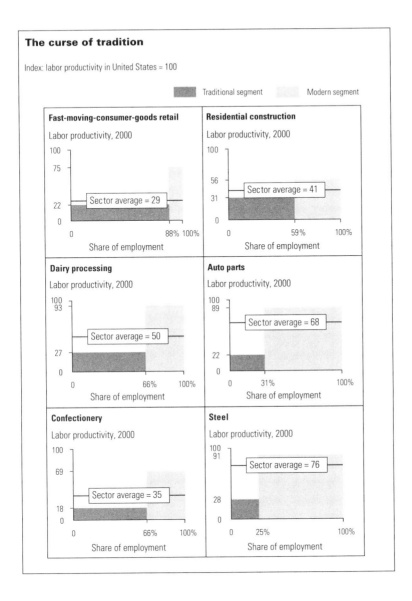

The curse of tradition

Index: labor productivity in United States = 100

Traditional segment   Modern segment

Fast-moving-consumer-goods retail

Labor productivity, 2000

Sector average = 29

Share of employment

Residential construction

Labor productivity, 2000

Sector average = 41

Share of employment

Dairy processing

Labor productivity, 2000

Sector average = 50

Share of employment

Auto parts

Labor productivity, 2000

Sector average = 68

Share of employment

Confectionery

Labor productivity, 2000

Sector average = 35

Share of employment

Steel

Labor productivity, 2000

Sector average = 76

Share of employment

petition, leads to high prices and dampened demand. The third reason for the underperformance is a lack of investment in technology. The state-owned wireline company Türk Telecom, for example, has failed to invest sufficiently in high-speed value-added services and hasn't automated its management of faults.

If the modern companies tackled these problems and raised their productivity to 95 percent of the levels of their US counterparts, the other half of the gap between Turkey's current and potential productivity levels could be closed.

Root causes

We have identified several causes of low productivity in both the traditional and the modern sectors, but companies aren't taking the necessary steps to correct the problem. Why don't modern companies invest more in technology, and why don't traditional ones upgrade their operations? The answer lies in the three underlying causes of Turkey's low productivity.

1. The informal economy

In Turkey as in other emerging economies, traditional companies that have failed to take measures to improve their performance are going out of business in the face of increased competition from more efficient players. Yet the scale of corporate failure is much more limited than would be expected given the extent of the operational inefficiency in sectors such as confectionery. The reason is that a lot of traditional companies derive a cost advantage by flouting tax, labor, and product market regulations. Many, for example, fail to remit value-added-tax (VAT) or social-security payments, to adhere to hygiene or product quality standards, or to pay minimum wages.

The size and impact of this cost advantage vary among industries. In the retailing of fast-moving consumer goods, not paying tax remittances could more than double a retailer's monthly income. That *isn't* enough in the long run to outweigh the overall cost advantage modern retailers enjoy thanks to their superior productivity. However, it is sufficient to enable some companies to survive a few more years even as turnover erodes. The low productivity of traditional retailers ought to imply a 10 or 20 percent annual decline in their numbers; the actual rate is 5 or 6 percent. In the dairy business, the bankruptcy rate is even lower, with some informal operators enjoying a cost advantage of as much as 20 percent, helping even the most inefficient to stay afloat.

Furthermore, the substantial cost advantages of the informal economy not only protect traditional firms from going out of business but also act as a disincentive to improving their productivity. For example, the Bakkalim project attempted by Migros Turk, the country's biggest grocery retailer, involved efforts to organize smaller stores under an umbrella brand that would give them extra purchasing, logistics, and merchandising muscle. Because membership required participants to comply with tax and social-security regulations, few grocers were willing to sign up.

Cracking down on informal operators does have a short-term cost: in developing countries, they provide work for large groups of unskilled laborers who migrate to urban centers, and many of these jobs could be lost. But in the long term, higher productivity would create far more jobs. We estimate that 33 percent of the gap between Turkey's current and potential productivity is due to the informal economy. No doubt, there would be a time lag between job losses and job creation, and the transition wouldn't be easy. Much of the pain could be ameliorated with targeted programs, however, and we contend that tackling the problem of the informal economy will pay very worthwhile long-term dividends.

Since we found no evidence in Turkey of regulatory loopholes that allow companies to avoid tax and other social obligations and to violate product market rules, the first step is to ensure stricter enforcement of existing laws. Poor enforcement is largely the result of weak processes and systems: tax offices are understaffed and poorly organized, for instance, and penalties for evasion negligible. Political decisions exacerbate the problem. Since 1963, Turkey has issued ten tax amnesties, most of which permitted delinquent parties who came forward to pay back taxes in installments *and* to use old Turkish lira values—a fabulous offer in a country where inflation averaged more than 60 percent a year during the 1990s. Not surprisingly, many people prefer to bide their time until the next tax amnesty rather than make their payments on time.

Bolstering enforcement of a range of regulations across many industries simultaneously would be a massive undertaking. It would be more practical to focus initially on a single area. We believe that this area should be tax evasion, which accounts for the largest portion of the informal operators' cost advantage. Moreover, better tax enforcement should enable the government to lower tax rates, thereby encouraging more companies to join the formal economy. In the retailing of fast-moving consumer goods, for example, the state collects only some 64 percent of the VAT revenue owed. If that could be increased to 90 percent, the VAT rate could be lowered to 13 percent, from 18 percent, with no decrease in state revenues.

Turkey should consider following the lead of Poland, which under strong pressure from the EU began tackling its informal economy in 1993 by focusing on VAT evasion in the retail sector. A combination of comprehensive audits, substantial monetary penalties, and, particularly, a change in cash register requirements to keep better track of sales had a significant impact, according to Polish experts.

If need be, Turkey could narrow its initial effort even further, to the retailing of fast-moving consumer goods. Enforcing VAT has the advantage that compliance by any single company makes enforcement possible both upstream and downstream.[8] The retailing of fast-moving consumer goods is an appropriate sector to choose not only because almost all retail outlets in Turkey are registered and thus easy to identify[9] but also because the product range within this sector is quite broad. As much as 20 percent of total Turkish economic activity is connected with it at some level.

Tougher enforcement of tax and social obligations and of product market regulations is the stick that will encourage traditional companies to join the formal economy and to modernize their operations. A carrot too is needed. Many small and mid-size enterprises lack the know-how to modernize, so government and private-enterprise associations ought to educate them. For a start, Turkey should aggressively exploit and even try to deepen the assistance the EU already offers to implement programs (styled after EU models) that help such companies improve their technology, increase their operating efficiency, and access export markets.

2. Macroeconomic and political instability

The sine qua non for sustained economic progress in Turkey is macroeconomic and political stability. Analysts have shown how the debilitating economic contractions of the past decade— too often caused by weak and short-lived governments—have led to high interest rates, high inflation, and high government debt. But the effect of economic instability on productivity has received little attention. Our study indicates that almost half of the gap between Turkey's current and potential productivity is due to economic volatility, which hurts modern companies most and largely accounts for their failure to improve business processes, their low capacity utilization, and their insufficient investment in technology.

Instability hampers productivity in three ways. First, high real interest rates often mean that more money can be made, more easily, from treasury operations than from productivity improvements, particularly in cash-oriented businesses. In the 1990s, real interest rates averaged around 20 percent but were frequently much higher; immediately after the currency devaluation in early 2001, they shot up to 90 percent.

"The allure of unearned income" demonstrates the importance of nonoperating income for a single large retailer and for retail banks. In 2001, when the Turkish economy contracted by almost 10 percent, this retailer earned no net income from operations but had $60 million in nonoperating income. Under these conditions, it is hard to blame a retailer's owner or manager for spending much more time negotiating payment terms with manufacturers

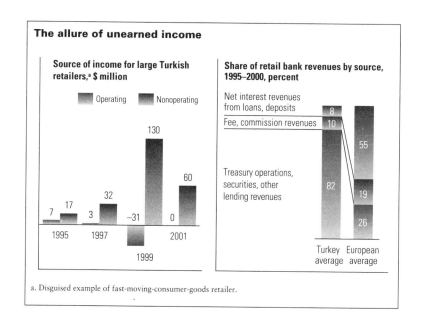

The allure of unearned income

Source of income for large Turkish retailers,[a] $ million

Operating / Nonoperating

130
60
32
17
7   3   −31   0
1995   1997   1999   2001

Share of retail bank revenues by source, 1995–2000, percent

Net interest revenues from loans, deposits
Fee, commission revenues
Treasury operations, securities, other lending revenues

	Turkey average	European average
Net interest revenues from loans, deposits	8	55
Fee, commission revenues	10	
Treasury operations, securities, other lending revenues	82	19
		26

a. Disguised example of fast-moving-consumer-goods retailer.

and managing cash than worrying about core operational improvements. We believe that this behavior, rather than a lack of management know-how, explains the limited use of advanced practices in the retail sector. In retail banking, most operators have made so much money from treasury operations that they haven't felt the need to become efficient in their core business.

The second effect of economic volatility is that high real interest rates make borrowing expensive, so investment in technology and automation is reduced; confectionery companies, for example, don't buy equipment to prepare dough or to automate packaging. And high real interest rates are a massive disincentive to borrowing for houses—Turkey has no mortgage market, because of prohibitively high (and volatile) real interest rates—and this problem weakens the construction industry.

Third, violent and sudden swings in demand make planning a nightmare; the automobile assembly and cement industries, for example, added substantial capacity in the late '80s and early '90s in anticipation of strong growth that never materialized. It is incredibly difficult to adjust labor and plant capacity effectively in the face of such macroeconomic uncertainty. After the financial crisis of 2001, loan activity was virtually nonexistent, but banks were reluctant to lay off employees, as they had no idea how long the crisis would last.

The MGI study doesn't aim to prescribe specific measures to stabilize Turkey's macroeconomic and political environment, though it should be noted that the financial prerequisites of macroeconomic stability are well understood and that loans from the International Monetary Fund are contingent upon them. However, this study should provide an incentive for sustained macroeconomic reforms, since it clearly demonstrates the enormous impact that a greater degree of stability would have on productivity and thus on economic growth.

3. Government ownership

Previous MGI work shows that, with few exceptions, state-owned enterprises are less productive than privately owned ones. In Turkey as elsewhere, managers in the state sector lack incentives to increase profits, while restructuring is politically difficult because of job losses. Our study found that government ownership accounted for one-sixth of the gap between Turkey's current and potential productivity.

The electricity and retail-banking sectors clearly suffer from excess labor, and retail banking and wireline telecommunications are held back because they don't experience enough pressure to offer new services that could increase output. The textbook response is privatization and liberalization, and Turkey has plans for both in the electricity, wireline telecom, and retail-banking sectors. To ensure the desired benefits, it will be important to stage and manage the transfer of assets within a carefully constructed regulatory framework. Particularly in telecommunications and electricity, the country's regulatory framework falls well below the bar.

Turkey's telecom industry provides a cautionary tale. The wireline sector has yet to be liberalized and suffers from a lack of incentives. Its productivity[10] stands at 66 percent of the US level. Startlingly, however, productivity in the liberalized wireless sector is actually lower—59 percent. Part of the reason was the bad design of liberalization: the government insisted that the second wave of new mobile license holders build base-station networks covering the entire country instead of ensuring that newcomers and incumbents signed roaming agreements. The result has been that much of the new capacity is now redundant, which has dragged down capital productivity.

This experience shouldn't deter Turkey from undertaking further privatization and liberalization; it just serves to emphasize that reform needs to be carried out carefully. If the government hits on the right combination of privatization and liberalization, we estimate that labor productivity could double in telecommunications and triple in electricity generation.

It's make-or-break time for Turkey. If it has the resolve to undertake the reforms outlined here, it can double the living standards of its people within a decade and move that much closer to fulfilling its dream of joining the EU. If it balks at the task, its economy will continue to underperform. The country has already come a long way, and many of its companies *have* become efficient and productive. It would be a terrible waste if Turkey now failed to grasp the opportunity to transform its entire economy.

Foreign investment: A poor record

Turkey's level of foreign direct investment (FDI) is lower in the sectors we studied than the level in many other emerging markets and much lower than one would expect for a country of its size and importance (see "Turkey's investment gap"). FDI is crucial not only because of its impact on the input side of the productivity equation but also because foreign companies usually force local ones to be more competitive.

It has been argued that the bureaucracy is to blame for Turkey's low FDI. Red tape can certainly be onerous; for example, 19 different administrative steps, several of them superfluous in the light of International standard practices, are required to establish a company. But our interviews suggest that this isn't a fundamental barrier to productivity: it affects all players, foreign and domestic alike, and therefore doesn't distort competitive intensity. Some foreign managers say that certain elements of red tape are just as bad elsewhere, both in developed and developing economies.

Instead, Turkey's poor record on foreign direct investment appears to be due to the same three factors that explain the country's low productivity. The Informal economy, for one thing, hampers foreign investors' growth prospects. Nestlé and Danone, for example, both invested in Turkey's dairy market after the liberalization of raw-milk sourcing, in the early 1990s, but capacity utilization in the modern producers' plants is almost 30 percent lower than the US average because informal players, with their unearned cost advantages, have clung to a disproportionate share of the market.

Moreover, the high real interest rates resulting from macroeconomic and political instability have warped investment decisions. Until very recently, foreign banks participated in the Turkish market only to a limited extent because of the high valuations Turkish banks enjoyed on the strength of their treasury profits. Foreign banks weren't prepared to pay such high prices to enter the market. Last, state ownership of capital-intensive sectors such as telecommunications and electricity has deterred foreign investors from putting their money into Turkey, though they *have* poured funds into the same sectors in other developing economies.

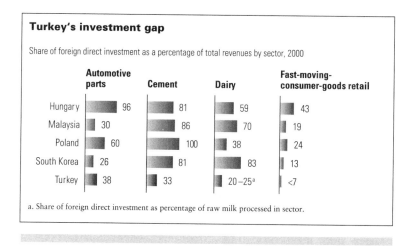

Turkey's investment gap

Share of foreign direct investment as a percentage of total revenues by sector, 2000

	Automotive parts	Cement	Dairy	Fast-moving-consumer-goods retail
Hungary	96	81	59	43
Malaysia	30	86	70	19
Poland	60	100	38	24
South Korea	26	81	83	13
Turkey	38	33	20–25[a]	<7

a. Share of foreign direct investment as percentage of raw milk processed in sector.

Didem Dincer Baser, Diana Farrell, and David E. Meen,
McKinsey Quarterly, 2003 Special Edition: Global directions.

Notes

1. Turkey currently has some 67 million people; the EU's most populous state, Germany, has 83 million. However, Germany's population is shrinking by about 82,000 a year, and Turkey's is growing rapidly. Turkey is expected to overtake Germany by 2014. If, as some expect, Turkey joins in 2007, along with Bulgaria and Romania, it will eventually be the EU's most populous state.

2. A full version of the study can be found at www.mckinsey.com.mgi.

3. The 11 sectors studied were apparel, automotive parts, cement, confectionery, dairy processing, electricity, residential construction, retail banking, the retailing of fast-moving consumer goods, steel, and telecommunications. Combined, they account for more than one-quarter of nonagricultural GDP and more than 30 percent of nonagricultural employment. They were chosen both to represent the aggregate utilities, services, and manufacturing sectors and because international benchmarks were available from earlier MGI studies. Unless stated otherwise, productivity refers to labor productivity.

4. Some productivity improvements aren't viable at Turkey's current consumer income and labor cost levels. Higher capital productivity can't be achieved in electricity, for example, because people don't consume enough of it at their current levels of income.

5. The Turkey-EU Customs Union came into force on January 1, 1996. Apart from Andorra, Malta, and San Marino, Turkey is the only nonmember state to sign such an agreement. Under it, the country has abolished tariff and nontariff protection against all EU goods it covers, is progressively moving toward the EU's common external tariff, and has been adopting the EU's preferential trade system through free-trade agreements with third-party countries. As of 1999, Turkey was the EU's 7th-biggest export destination (up from 9th in 1990) and the 13th-biggest exporter to the EU (up from 17th in 1990).

6. The study revealed two distinct clusters of companies. "Traditional" is the label we gave to those with exceptionally low levels of

productivity. A search for commonalities to explain this phenomenon revealed one broad characteristic: all traditional companies use business processes and technologies that are at least two, and often three or four, generations behind current state-of-the-art practices. "Modern" companies in our study have productivity levels two to three times higher than those of the traditional companies. Almost invariably, modern companies use business practices that are much closer to the state of the art.

7. Productivity among traditional companies would reach its potential as a result of two things. First, certain companies would modernize. As the benchmark for their potential, we used the current productivity of US small and midsize enterprises. Second, some output would shift to more efficient operators as companies that failed to modernize went out of business. Consult the full MGI report for more details of the methodology.

8. Businesses remit net VAT payments—that is, the difference between the VAT they receive from their customers and the VAT their suppliers receive from them. Thus, they identify sales from wholesalers, and wholesalers identify sales from manufacturers, which in turn identify raw-material providers.

9. In contrast to tax enforcement, conducted at the state level, the enforcement of the obligation to register businesses (for a relatively small charge) is strict, partly because the responsibility lies with municipalities that want to maximize receipts under their control.

10. In telecommunications, we use a measure of total factor productivity—that is, labor productivity and capital productivity.

7

Asia: the productivity imperative

Diana Farrell

IDEAS IN BRIEF

Even in the divergent economies of India, Japan, Korea, and Thailand, they share important similarities in how to achieve greater prosperity.

Raising productivity in sectors where productivity is comparatively low has the potential to increase economic growth significantly.

In domestically oriented industries, levels of Asian labor productivity are a fraction of US levels, and regulations inadvertently restrict competitive intensity.

This chapter is based on the following four country studies the McKinsey Global Institute has prepared over the last few years: *India: The Growth Imperative* (September 2001); *Why the Japanese Economy Is Not Growing* (July 2000); *Productivity-Led Growth for Korea* (March 1998); and *Thai Productivity Report: Prosperity through Productivity* (February 2002). The latter represents a joint project undertaken by McKinsey's Thailand office, supported by the MGI in collaboration with two leading Thai economic research think tanks: the National Economic and Social Development Board (NESDB) and the Thai Development Research Institute Foundation (TDRI).

Japan's economic stagnation during the 1990s and the economic crisis across Asia in 1997–1998 raised serious questions about how the region could build on its former economic success. Earlier strategies seemed to be running out of steam. Policymakers needed something different to attain sustainable growth.

The McKinsey Global Institute (MGI) examined the region's potential closely in the early years of this decade, studying a wide range of industries to identify alternative routes to growth. Making meaningful generalizations about a region so diverse is a challenge. Not only does Asia account for a good portion of the world's population, but different countries were pursuing different economic strategies. That said, however, our examination of four apparently divergent economies—those of India, Japan, Korea, and Thailand—revealed important similarities in how they might achieve greater prosperity.

Japan and Korea had been relying on ever increasing inputs of capital and labor to drive higher economic output. India and Thailand, on the other hand, were competing largely on their comparative advantages in production factors, especially their labor costs and natural resources. But the "input-driven" economies were experiencing diminishing returns on investment, while the "factor advantaged" were being challenged by other economies with superior advantages—China in particular. In all four economies, however, our studies showed that focusing on raising productivity in those sectors where their productivity levels were comparatively low had the potential to increase economic growth significantly.

Each of these economies had some sectors that were relatively efficient and productive, and some that were the opposite. Our studies found that the dividing line was—and remains—no accident. Asia's export-led growth has ensured that its export industries have been subject to the forces of rigorous market competition. In these industries, labor productivity is relatively high. In contrast, those industries and services that are domestically oriented—the non-tradable sectors—have faced less competition and their productivity growth has lagged. In the domestically oriented industries that we studied, we found levels of Asian labor productivity to be a fraction of US levels. It is here that the opportunity lies.

A pressing need that all these countries face is to increase productivity in the domestic, non-tradable sectors of their economies. In traded sectors, like consumer electronics or automotive, international competition defines the type of goods and services required, and their attributes. Domestically oriented industries and services, in contrast, are largely shaped by domestic conditions. Unfortunately, these conditions are frequently set by inappropriate regulations, which have tended to ossify industry structures rather than increase productivity. So the challenge for these countries is to emulate the rigors of international market competition in their domestic, non-tradable sectors.

The local nature of the forces shaping competition in domestic-oriented industries means that each country's requirements are likely to be fairly unique or, at the very least, will exhibit unique characteristics. Food, housing, and retailing are all subject to national tastes, culture, and demands. But that makes it neither impossible nor undesirable to improve productivity in these industries. Although, almost by definition, domestic goods and services cannot be physically traded, less direct forms of international competition can be encouraged, better methods and technologies can be introduced, and markets can be reshaped. And in other parts of the world, productivity gains have been achieved in domestic sectors without sacrificing national tastes, culture, and demands (although those with vested interests in protecting the status quo are likely to exaggerate the threat of such a sacrifice). So there is nothing inevitable about, say, the low productivity of Japanese retailing, or Korean housing. Nor is it inevitable that making Japanese retailing more productive would make it un-Japanese, or that efficient Korean housing would be somehow not Korean.

Asia's policymakers nevertheless have to make difficult tradeoffs to realize the productivity gains their economies need. This article highlights some of these tradeoffs. It sketches the challenges policymakers face and the decisions they need to make. We use data from the housing construction and retail sectors in India, Japan, Korea, and Thailand to illustrate the significant economic cost of certain product, market, and land regulations, and the costs of failing to enforce more beneficial regulations.

We examine the opportunities for improving productivity and how policymakers can help to realize them.

Regulations that stifle competition

How is it that well intentioned regulations end up inhibiting overall productivity growth in an economy? Our work in Asia suggests they do so by inadvertently restricting competitive intensity in non-tradable sectors. Regulations can do this in a number of ways, ranging from preventing consolidation—including preventing players in an industry from reaching the scale where automation becomes possible—to promoting collaborative rather than competitive relationships that substantially limit the desire among players to adopt new, more productive practices.

The problems of the non-tradable sector often interlock, explaining in part why reform has proved so difficult and productivity improvements so elusive. In Japan, for instance, the regulations restricting competition among large-scale retailers interact with those that inadvertently provide incentives to small-scale retailers not to exit the industry. The resulting fragmentation in the retail sector has the knock-on effect of preventing consolidation in the food processing industry. The same tax incentives that discourage small-scale retailers from exiting also prevent large-scale housing construction in Japan. As a result, the housing construction industry remains sub-scale and there is little to drive Design for Manufacturing (DFM) processes or standardization of materials.

For reform to succeed, it clearly needs to tackle the interlocking nature of the underlying obstacles to productivity improvement. The nature of the housing construction and retail industries in our four case economies illustrate how regulations can themselves become or create such obstacles.

Housing construction

Families are very important in Asia and the home is central to the family. Moreover, housing expresses tradition: whole regions and even countries are identified with traditional forms of domestic architecture. Both factors make housing precious, and local regulation often aims to protect its unique characteristics. But it has not been entirely successful. Modern houses in India, Japan, Korea, and Thailand have much more in common with each other than with the traditional forms of housing in any of these countries. Modernity has already won in terms of construction form.

However, efficiency has not come hand in hand with modernity. We observed a very wide range of productivity levels in housing construction across the countries studied, from 8 percent of US levels in India to 69 percent in Korea. With the exception of India, where the very low levels of income of large sections of the population constrain the potential for productivity to improve, productivity in the other countries could potentially reach around 90 percent of US levels. By way of comparison, the Netherlands has labor productivity levels comparable with those seen in the United States, and has arguably been more successful than most other countries in integrating modern construction with its traditional urban landscape. Efficiency and tradition are not contradictory.

We studied housing construction in detail in Japan, Korea, and India. The sector is a critical contributor to each economy, accounting for between 1 and 5 percent of GDP and between 1 and 4 percent of employment (see "Size of housing construction industry"). The sector also meets a basic social need. Improve-

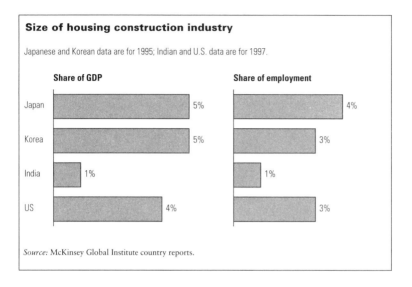

Size of housing construction industry

Japanese and Korean data are for 1995; Indian and U.S. data are for 1997.

Share of GDP

Japan	5%
Korea	5%
India	1%
US	4%

Share of employment

Japan	4%
Korea	3%
India	1%
US	3%

Source: McKinsey Global Institute country reports.

ments in housing construction therefore have a direct impact on improving individual well-being and aggregate standards of living: few would argue against lower housing prices and making affordable housing more widely available.

Housing construction is non-tradable, because of the many obstacles hampering the transfer of construction technology, systems, skills, and knowledge between markets. These include differences in safety and planning regulation, climate, local expectations of housing densities and housing forms, and house buyers' product expectations. To succeed in the industry requires access to a vast amount of hard and soft information and deep knowledge of local operating conditions. As a result, housing construction is one of the few markets where foreign firms are loath to enter, even if the market is fully open.

If policymakers cannot look to foreign firms to provide competition in housing construction, what else can they do to improve its productivity? Our analysis of the industry suggests that they should work on two key causes of low productivity in housing construction: the range of different types of housing available, or the product mix; and the degree of price competition.

Product mix

Individual house buyers are generally presented with a limited set of housing options within their price range. However, the potential set of options is much wider. Changes in the product mix can either increase the value of housing or lower construction costs or both, yielding substantial productivity improvements. To understand how, we examine the four dimensions of choice that determine the prevailing product mix in a national housing market.

1. *Single family or multi-family housing?* Multi-family housing, such as apartments, condominiums, or flats, is higher density and uses land more efficiently but, typically, it creates lower value added per unit, which translates into lower productivity. Korea has a high percentage of multi-family housing because zoning and regulations capping housing prices limit the amount of available land. Multi-family housing accounts for 81 percent of all new construction in Korea, compared with only 20 percent in the United States. However, Korean single-family housing is 56 percent more productive than its multi-family housing counterpart.

Although this is a common pattern, for a number of reasons Japan is an exception to the rule. It has a fairly high percentage of multi-family housing, which comprises a little over half of all new construction. In Japan, such housing is slightly more productive than single-family housing. However, it is still only 60 percent as productive as US levels (see "Comparison of housing mix, 1999").

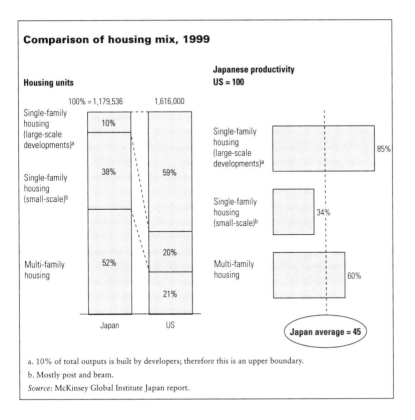

Comparison of housing mix, 1999

a. 10% of total outputs is built by developers; therefore this is an upper boundary.
b. Mostly post and beam.
Source: McKinsey Global Institute Japan report.

If land prices are high, surely more multi-family housing is the right solution for Korea? Only if the problem being solved is how to build more cheap housing. But in richer markets, the right question to ask is how can housing construction create the greatest value. Looking at the problem in this light makes it clear that there are alternative approaches to the current multi-family constructions, because house buyers in Korea are looking for "good value." Good value might well derive, for example, from a higher price for a single family dwelling. Alternatively, it might derive from better shared amenities in a multi-family dwelling, such as shops, a gymnasium, or a swimming pool. The price of inputs into the product mix is also not necessarily static. For instance, though land prices are high, Korea's zoning regulation keeps them higher than they may need to be.

Experience elsewhere in the world, such as in the Netherlands, shows that well planned single-family units can also be relatively high density, and that improved transport infrastructure can quickly revalue otherwise unpopular locations. The garden suburb is not a one-size-fits-all solution, but neither is the multi-family skyscraper. Greater productivity in housing can be achieved by imaginative use of the land available and by making a wider variety of options available to home buyers.

2. *Primary or secondary market?* The prevalence of the secondary housing market—the market for "used homes"—is the second determinant of the product mix in a local housing market. In both Japan and India, the secondary housing market is very weak. Some would argue that the lack of a secondary housing market is a good thing, in that societies where people own only one house in a lifetime are probably highly stable, with strong community bonds. The reverse side of extreme social stability, however, is an extreme lack of social mobility.

In the United States, 66 percent of all housing moves are within the same area and only 10 percent are caused by job relocation, suggesting that fulfilling personal aspirations plays a large part in shaping the secondary housing market there. One outcome of this is that each house in the United States undergoes 17 times as many transactions as does the average Japanese house, and each transaction creates value for the economy.

India and Japan have not developed a secondary housing market for two main reasons: information transparency and tax disincentives. In both countries, there is insufficient information relevant to transactions, particularly about market prices and quality. Buyers and sellers therefore find it difficult to agree on a price, as there is no objective way of measuring what premium to the going market price, if any, is being asked. Similarly, in both countries transaction taxes deter owners from selling. In Japan the tax structure strongly discourages short-term ownership: a tax of 40 percent is imposed on capital gains from properties owned for less than five years, compared with 14 percent for those owned for more than ten years.

3. *Large-scale or small-scale construction?* Economies of scale in housing construction come from the efficient use of prefabricated materials, better equipment utilization, bulk purchasing of materials, and spreading architecture fees. Together, such economies can reduce construction costs by 25 percent as when, for example, a contractor builds 50 single-family row homes at once, rather than constructing single units, one by one.

Achieving such economies of scale depends on a contractor being able to construct housing in large volumes, and on standardization. Large volumes are the result of large-scale investment. Smaller builders are not typically in a position to realize these economies. Standardization results from regulations that require it, or from largescale construction, or the two acting in combination.

Unfortunately, conditions in each of the housing markets did not favor economies of scale. There was neither much large-scale construction nor standardization, limiting the opportunity for skills and systems transfer. In Japan, for example, there are some 150 regional systems or standards for the construction of traditional post-and-beam housing, and 10 systems even for prefabricated housing. In more productive markets, DFM has shaped construction because of the way it influences planning and changes the task of the housing contractor from a craft to an assembly job. The use of standardized materials in doors and windows, plumbing and wiring, flooring and roofing, and wall and roof components means tasks can be specialized, and installation time reduced.

In India, large-scale, standardized construction is difficult for two reasons. First, the underlying infrastructure is poorly developed, so "green-field" sites are relatively unattractive to developers. Second, high population densities and fragmented land ownership patterns mean that there is, in any case, a shortage of suitable land for development. Japan faces similar constraints. The supply of suitable land plots for large-scale construction is limited because of the high taxes on property sales mentioned earlier (the property and inheritance tax), and land fragmentation caused by urban development laws. So in both India and Japan, it would be difficult achieve the benefits of scale without changes in policy.

4. *Higher or lower quality?* In much of the Asian housing market, construction quality is lower than prices might suggest. In Japan, for example, high levels of design customization combined with a shortage of the requisite skills in areas such as carpentry and joinery has led to inefficient design and a relatively low quality of execution. The 1998 Survey on the Demand for Housing conducted by the Japanese Ministry of Construction found that 48 percent of all households were dissatisfied with their housing conditions, because of the lack of provision for the elderly, poor soundproofing and insulation, inadequate space, high levels of wear and tear, and inadequate air-conditioning and water supply. Market constraints mean that there is insufficient higher-quality property available in both Japan and Korea, the market mix favoring the lower end. Again, this reduces the potential value each worker can add in construction.

These shortcomings are all largely the result of well-intended regulation. In Korea, for instance, price caps on housing, intended to protect lower-income groups, mean builders deliver lower quality to stay within the price constraints. Korean construction firms supply just the bare walls, whereas in the United States builders will add a large number of fixtures and fittings, such as refrigerators, ovens, fireplaces, carpets, and the like. Approximately one-third of the productivity gap between Korea and the United States is accounted for by differences in quality and content mix.

Price competition

The other major factor determining the productivity of the housing construction sector is the level of price competition. In all the markets we studied, price competition for contractors and developers was easily disrupted, and direct incentives to improve productivity in the industry thus reduced. The lack of information transparency in India and Japan, for example, prevents house buyers from making like for like price comparisons. This gives contractors considerable power in shaping the production outcome, especially because standards for materials and construction methods are inadequately enforced. In India, for example, this allows contractors to focus on procuring the cheapest materials they can, but without passing on their cost savings to the home buyer. As a result, materials are often of poor or of substandard quality, and contractors have profit levels substantially higher than the international average. Developers and contractors collude in materials procurement but neglect site design or project management.

In both India and Japan, competition between developers primarily takes the form of securing access to land, as opposed to price-based competition. Large-scale land plots are seldom available. When they are, such competition is intense, because whoever controls the land controls the market. Although this is true to a large extent elsewhere in the world, it is important to recognize that a poorly functioning land market worsens the lack of price transparency.

What needs to be done?

Housing construction represents a set of interlocking problems that are unlikely to be unraveled independently. The product mix and level of price competition have been shaped by a number of historical factors that hold down productivity. Policymakers need to consider what they can do to unlock this logjam. However, changes cannot be made without tradeoffs. Measures to improve the housing mix and sharpen price competition need to be taken in the context of the economy as a whole.

That said, two key interventions could raise labor productivity in housing construction in these countries: creating the scale to optimize DFM techniques, and achieving greater transparency in pricing. Current barriers to scale prevent the introduction and use of DFM techniques. The resulting lack of standardization and inefficiency of design leads to significantly lower productivity. The lack of standardization also makes it difficult to achieve price transparency, as individual houses vary so much in their methods of construction, in their design, and in the quality of materials used to build them.

Policymakers need to examine the housing mix in the light of the need to remove obstacles to scale in the industry. The right strategy could enable well-funded developers simultaneously to develop large-scale housing projects and adopt DFM, better project management, and standardized materials.

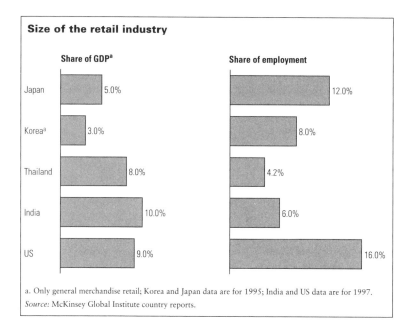

Size of the retail industry

a. Only general merchandise retail; Korea and Japan data are for 1995; India and US data are for 1997.
Source: McKinsey Global Institute country reports.

Retail

The challenges to retail productivity in Asia are similar to those facing housing construction. Firstly, retail is a very large and important sector of Asia's economies, representing between 5 and 10 percent of each nation's GDP and from 6 to 16 percent of its employment (see "Size of the retail industry"). Secondly, there is a large productivity gap compared with the United States. Although we observed a wide range of productivity levels across the countries studied, none reached a level more than half that of the United States. Thirdly, the retail industry is subject to many of the same cultural and regulatory pressures as housing construction.

Because retail is essentially linked to personal, regional, and national consumption preferences, it is harder for policymakers to make reforms in this sector than in those less in the public eye.

Retail reform has a definite impact on the lifestyle and behaviors of individuals. As with housing construction, however, growth in the retail sector is driven by increasing consumption, which is likely to be considered a positive development by the public at large.

Improving productivity in retailing contributes to wider productivity improvement because more efficient retailers put pressure on upstream suppliers to improve their productivity too. Productivity improvements in retail are also highly visible, as they tend to be translated quickly into lower retail prices. This in turn stimulates demand and raises the standard of living across the economy.

Modern retail format

The low productivity of the retail sector in Asia stems primarily from the limited share of modern retail formats in the sector and the continuing reliance on traditional store formats (see "Size and productivity of traditional and modern retail industry"). In

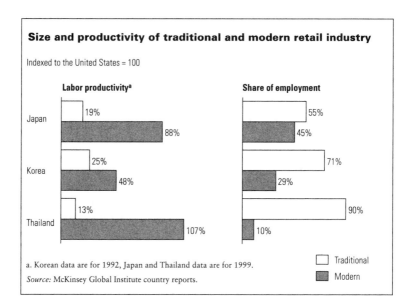

Size and productivity of traditional and modern retail industry

Indexed to the United States = 100

	Labor productivity[a]	Share of employment
Japan — Traditional	19%	55%
Japan — Modern	88%	45%
Korea — Traditional	25%	71%
Korea — Modern	48%	29%
Thailand — Traditional	13%	90%
Thailand — Modern	107%	10%

a. Korean data are for 1992, Japan and Thailand data are for 1999.
Source: McKinsey Global Institute country reports.

☐ Traditional
▨ Modern

Japan, for example, the productivity gap between Japanese discounters and general merchandise stores and those in the United States is negligible. However, Japan's discounters account for only 12 percent of retail employment in Japan, compared with 35 percent in the United States. In contrast, the share of employment derived from traditional stores in Japan is 55 percent compared with 19 percent in the United States, while productivity is only 33 percent of the US levels of "mom and pop" stores.

Of course, what is considered to be traditional varies widely between countries, from wet markets in Thailand to street vendors in India to small local stores in Korea and Japan. There are two sets of factors that explain traditional stores' continuing dominance throughout Asia: factors that reduce the competitive position of modern formats relative to traditional formats, and policies that bar the entry of modern formats.

1. *Factors that reduce the competitive position of modern formats.* These typically provide an artificial cost advantage to traditional retailers. In Thailand and India, these advantages take the form of a combination of regulatory "special treatment" for traditional retailers, and weak enforcement of regulations that they should observe. As a result, traditional retailers can pay less tax and skirt minimum wage requirements. In India, underdeveloped upstream industries also add costs and complicate sourcing for modern formats, preventing them from reaching the levels of scale and standardization necessary for higher productivity. In Japan, low property taxes, high capital gains taxes, and inheritance tax reductions discourage traditional retailers from exiting and selling off land. Government loan guarantees and subsidies also help support the position of traditional retailers in Japan.

2. *Policies that prevent the entry of modern retail formats.* A shortage of available land is one of the biggest barriers to entry in retail in all the countries examined. In India, the scarcity of appropriate real estate for modern formats is due to generous tenancy rights, and also unclear land titles, which make land transactions lengthy and complex. In Japan, the large-scale retail location law essentially allows local traditional retailers to limit the entry of large-scale retailers in their area. In Korea, restrictive zoning and land development laws restrict the use of land and reduce its availability, especially for large buildings such as shopping malls.

Additionally, explicit or implicit restrictions on foreign direct investment (FDI) also inhibit the entry of modern format retailers and the introduction of best practices. In Korea, for example, FDI is forbidden in department stores and shopping malls. Complicated and time-consuming processes for applying to enter the Korean market are an additional deterrent. As a result of this restricted competition, even where modern formats do exist, they frequently exhibit fairly low levels of productivity because they lack exposure to best practice skills and methods. This is certainly the case in India, where there are explicit bans on FDI in the retail sector.

What needs to be done?

Quite simply, policy needs to encourage greater competitive intensity. This will in turn lead to a greater focus on more specialized merchandizing to meet the needs of defined consumer segments. For example, traditional stores have faced intense competition from large chains in France, but they continue to survive next door to supermarkets, by specializing as gourmet cheese stores, fresh-from-the-farm vegetable stores, ethnic grocery stores, patisseries, and the like. In Japan, the lack of merchandizing in traditional stores accounts for more than two-thirds of their productivity gap compared with US traditional stores (the remainder mainly derives from the absence of point-of-sale information technology).

Greater competitive intensity would clearly encourage the migration to more productive retail formats, because the more productive stores could pass on their cost savings in the form of lower prices, and thus win greater market share. In Japan, though large and regional supermarkets exhibit respectable levels of productivity, some 70 percent of supermarket employment is still in small, local stores. Their productivity is just 65 percent that of the larger Japanese supermarkets (and barely half US levels). They can remain inefficient largely because of the current regulatory framework, but this works against the interests of the mass of consumers.

Regulators may argue that protecting small retailers helps to meet local consumer preferences. However, increasing competitive intensity need not eliminate local stores. Rather, it can stimulate them to focus more productively on consumer needs. High productivity is not synonymous with complete uniformity—far from it—but it certainly is synonymous with greater competition.

The experience of Thailand's retail industry shows what a change in regulation can achieve. Overall, the level of Thailand's retail sector productivity, at 20 percent that of the United States, does not appear particularly encouraging, but this figure hides a more interesting story. Modern formats are in the process of transforming the industry. On average, their productivity level is 91 percent of that of similar formats in the United States, but labor productivity in Thailand's supermarkets is an encouraging

122 percent of US levels, and space efficiency, in terms of value added per square meter, an outstanding 210 percent of US levels. Modern formats now account for 44 percent of retail sales, and their penetration has been growing at an annual rate of 3.3 percent over the past 12 years. Although they account for only 10 percent of retail employment in Thailand, this too is changing fast. All this has been achieved in very few years, through a rapid revision of the retail regulations. The Asian financial crisis in 1997 prompted the government to liberalize FDI regulation in the retail industry and to allow enterprises with 100 percent foreign control from then on. This led to a dramatic increase in the intensity of competition, as seven multinational retailers entered the market. As a result, the proportion of sales of modern formats rose from 5 percent to 44 percent in just 12 years.

The productivity imperative

How to ensure that productivity continues to rise in Asia's economies is one of their policymakers' biggest challenges. On the one hand, countries at an early stage in the demographic shift, such as India and Thailand, have burgeoning populations. They will have plenty of people available for work: by 2010, as much as 62 percent of India's population will be aged between 15 and 59. The danger, however, is that labor productivity will fall. In contrast, Japan and Korea's populations are aging rapidly. The number of 15- to 64-year-olds in Japan will decline by 0.5 percent per year between 2000 and 2010. This will make Japan highly reliant on productivity improvements, rather than more labor, to sustain its standard of living.

Asian economies need to realize the kind of productivity improvements seen in recent years in tradable goods and services in their domestic non-tradable sectors. That will depend on regulatory reform to encourage more competition and stimulate investment. Legislators need to make difficult tradeoffs between conflicting objectives: the impact of changing restrictions on land ownership in Japan and Korea, raising FDI limits in India, and removing tariff and other domestic protections in Thailand are all cases in point.

Typically, reforms that remove restrictions that have been impeding competition in an industry allow a rapid influx of capital, often FDI, which can reshape the industry. International best practices, for instance, ranging from DEM in the housing construction industry and improved supply chain management and marketing in retail, can help to improve productivity greatly in any national industry. However, the nature of the non-tradable sector means that FDI cannot play this role in every one.

There is nothing to suggest that India, Korea, Japan, and Thailand cannot dramatically improve their productivity performance. On the contrary, our work suggests that the right kind of reforms to product market regulations will go a long way to close Asia's productivity gaps with global best practice. Without such action, however, productivity in the region's non-tradable industries is likely to remain much the same, putting Asia's economic well-being at risk.

Diana Farrell,
McKinsey Global Institute, 2003.

8

China and India:
the race to growth

**Diana Farrell, Jayant Sinha, Tarun Khanna, and
Jonathan R. Woetzel**

IDEAS IN BRIEF

The contrasting ways in which China and India are developing,
and the particular difficulties each still faces, prompt debate
about whether one country has a better approach to economic
development and will eventually emerge as the stronger.

China has shackled its independent businessmen, while India
has empowered them.

In an efficient market, the private sector is better than
governments at allocating investment funds. But China isn't an
efficient market, and India has relatively little investment funding.

The strength of the Chinese and Indian economies will actually
be decided at the industry level.

Firstit it was China. The rest of the world looked on in disbelief, then awe, as the Chinese economy began to take off in the 1980s at what seemed like lightning speed and the country positioned itself as a global economic power. GDP growth, driven largely by manufacturing, rose to 9 percent in 2003 after reaching 8 percent in 2002. China used its vast reservoirs of domestic savings to build an impressive infrastructure and sucked in huge amounts of foreign money to build factories and to acquire the expertise it needed. In 2003 it received $53 billion in foreign direct investment (FDI), or 8.2 percent[1] of the world's total—more than any other country.

India began its economic transformation almost a decade after China did but has recently grabbed just as much attention, prompted largely by the number of jobs transferred to it from the West. At the same time, the country is rapidly creating world-class businesses in knowledge-based industries such as software, IT services, and pharmaceuticals. These companies, which emerged with little government assistance, have helped propel the economy: GDP growth stood at 8.3 percent in 2003, up from 4.3 percent in 2002. But India's level of FDI— $4.7 billion in 2003, up from $3 billion in 2002—is a fraction of China's.

Both countries still have serious problems: India has poor roads and insufficient water and electricity supplies, all of which could thwart its development; China has massive bad bank loans that will have to be accounted for. The contrasting ways in

which China and India are developing, and the particular difficulties each still faces, prompt debate about whether one country has a better approach to economic development and will
eventually emerge as the stronger. We recently asked three leading experts for their views on the subject.

India's entrepreneurial advantage

Tarun Khanna

China and India have followed radically different approaches to
economic development. China's resulted from a conscious decision;
India more or less happened upon its course. Is one way better than
the other? There is no gainsaying the fact that China's growth has
rocketed ahead of India's, but the conventional view that the Chinese
model is unambiguously the better of the two is wrong in many ways;
each has its advantages. And it is far from clear which will deliver the
more sustainable growth.

Together with Yasheng Huang, of the Sloan School of Management, at the Massachusetts Institute of Technology (MIT), I have
argued that these approaches differ on two dimensions. First, the
Chinese government nurtures and directs economic activity more
than the Indian government does. It invests heavily in physical
infrastructure and often decides which companies—not
necessarily the best—receive government resources and listings
on local stock markets. By contrast, since the mid-1980s the
Indian government has become less and less interventionist. The
second dimension is FDI. China has embraced it; India remains
cautious.

These differences have an impact on the types of companies that
succeed and, I would argue, on entrepreneurialism. Let's look first at

what kinds of companies thrive. China trumps India when it comes to industries that rely on "hard" infrastructure (roads, ports, power) and will do so for the foreseeable future. But when it comes to "soft" infrastructure businesses—those in which intangible assets matter more—India tends to come out ahead, be it in software, biotechnology, or creative industries such as advertising.

Thus manufacturing companies whose just-in-time production processes rely on efficient road and transport networks fare poorly in India. But businesses that are unconstrained by shortages of generators and roads flourish. Soft assets underpin even the Indian car industry. Unlike China's car sector, which has expanded as a result of big capital investments from multinational companies, India's has succeeded on the back of clever designs that make it possible to produce cheap indigenous models. India actually sends China high-value-added mechanized and electronic components whose production depends more on know-how than on infrastructure.

Moreover, many hard-asset companies in China exist because the government funnels money to them. The government can do this because it intervenes in domestic capital markets. In India there is no such government intervention. Hence successful companies tend to cluster in industries where capital constraints are less of an issue. You don't need a deep reservoir of capital to start a software company; you do for a big steel plant.

The Indian government's lower level of intervention in capital markets and its decision not to regulate industries that lack tangible assets (software, biotech, media) have created room for entrepreneurs. Entrepreneurial activity is fueled both by incumbent (often family-owned) enterprises and by new entrants. The former use cash flows from diverse existing businesses to invest in newer ventures. In biotechnology, however, Biocon emerged from pure entrepreneurial effort, as did Infosys Technologies in software. Similarly, hundreds of smaller versions of companies such as Infosys and Wipro Technologies have no government links, unlike so many of China's successful companies.

Although India's stock and bond markets are hardly perfect, they do on the whole support private enterprise. Here too, entrepreneurialism has played a part, even improving India's institutional framework. Take the Bombay Stock Exchange (BSE), founded about 130 years ago and until recently the most inefficient entity imaginable. It has become radically more efficient in the past decade as a result of the competing efforts of an enterprising former bureaucrat named R. H. Patil. With technological inputs from around the world and some fancy footwork to dodge entrenched interests at the BSE, in 1994 he started a rival institution, the state-of-the-art National Stock Exchange of India, which now has more business. In China, by contrast, the government tries to make stock markets successful by command, with predictably little to show for its efforts. There has been little competition indeed between the Shanghai and Shenzhen exchanges.

Good hard infrastructure and the Chinese government's decision to welcome foreign investment make it reasonably easy for multinationals to do business in China, and since they bring their own capital and senior talent, they do not have to rely heavily on local institutions. China has no shortage of homegrown entrepreneurial talent. But indigenous companies have a much tougher time, hindered as they are by inefficient capital markets, a banking system notorious for bad loans, and the fact that local officials rather than market forces largely decide who receives funding.

China and India both have the ability to keep growing in their own very different ways for a decade or so. The Chinese government's intervention in the economy—including the decision to welcome foreign direct investment—has brought a material improvement in the standard of living that India hasn't enjoyed. It may also be that each country has chosen the path best suited to its own historical circumstances. But the pros and cons of these two development models should be studied, and it is fair to ask whether China's approach will hamper its future economic development.

Huang and I believe that the presence of so many self-reliant multi-national companies has partly relieved the Chinese government of pressure to develop or reform the institutions that support free enterprise and economic growth. And the fact that many domestic investments still are not allocated through sensible pricing mechanisms means that China wastes many of its resources. Productivity and long-term economic growth, as we all know, thrive on competition, which is all too often stifled by government intervention.

When the two countries are compared, it is easy to forget that India began its economic reforms more than a decade later than China did. As India opens up further to foreign direct investment, we might well discover that the country's more laissez-faire approach has nurtured the conditions that will enable free enterprise and economic growth to flourish more easily in the long run.

China: The best of all possible models

Jonathan R. Woetzel

Finding fault with China's approach to economic development is easy: cyclical overcapacity, state-influenced resource allocation, and growing social inequalities are just a few of its shortcomings. But it's hard to see how any other model could have given the economy such a powerful kick start.

The Chinese government manages the development of enterprises with a view to driving economic growth. You can be a small entrepreneur in China, but if you want to be big you will have to get money from a government-affiliated source at some point. Government officials essentially have the power to decide which companies grow.

In achieving the objective of growth, this policy has been tremendously successful. China has quickly built industries large enough to drive its economy. Take the auto industry, now an important contributor to the manufacturing sector. Only 20 years ago, China had no auto industry to speak of; there were a few manufacturers of trucks but none of passenger cars. To get started, the government decided that in a high-scale, high-tech industry, some foreign company—in this case, Volkswagen—had to come in and show local ones what to do. Because most local companies were state-owned 20 years ago, Volkswagen was hooked up with a state-owned company.

You might argue that this development model has thwarted entrepreneurship. But there weren't any entrepreneurs in the industry at the time. There were no private companies that could partner with Volkswagen, let alone compete with it. The government simply said, "We want China to modernize. We want the Chinese economy to grow. We don't have the companies we need to make that happen, so we're prepared to do what it takes to create them."

The capital-intensive auto plants built with foreign partners in China as a result of its development policy may have no particular productivity advantage over the plants they might have built at home. But all of the spending by the big car companies has paid off.

Moreover, local, privately owned automakers such as Chery Automotive and Geely Automotive are beginning to thrive. A generation of entrepreneurs has put to good advantage the skills and training that the foreigners provided, so that Chinese companies now put together cars of reasonable quality much more cheaply than foreign automakers can. At present, domestic players benefit from the price umbrella that the foreign ones provide. But these smaller fry are now making cars for $2,000, which means that any company that has high cost structures will eventually suffer. With lower tariffs on the way because of China's accession to the World Trade Organization, and with new competitors proliferating, the automotive industry is heading into a classic price war that only the fittest will survive. This is precisely what happened in the consumer electronics industry, where competition led to the emergence of successful Chinese companies that operate globally. I think that in five or ten years' time, at least a third of the Chinese auto industry will be completely private—nothing to do with the current state players. And this will all have started with the state saying, "We want to build a car industry." Looking at industry more broadly, inefficiencies and cyclicality have resulted from the fact that many funding decisions are driven at the local-government level. Local officials have GDP growth as a political-performance target, so many of them look for the biggest investments they can make to push along the regional economy. Like stock market investors pursuing the latest speculative fad, they have created a lemming effect, with lots of unsound investments, whether in aluminum smelters, residential real estate, or TV factories. The outcome tends to be waves of overcapacity as investments are made right up to—and sometimes way beyond—the point where it is patently obvious that the economics cannot justify them.

But remember that the essential mechanism of economic reform in China has been the encouragement of competition among provinces and municipalities. Until the 1980s there was no such thing in China as a national company. Everything was local. There was no single legal entity that operated more than five kilometers (about 3.1 miles) from its headquarters. With the removal of internal trade barriers, local entrepreneurs and their government backers invested to build scale and attack neighboring markets. Yes, this does lead to overcapacity and price wars. But over time—and relatively short periods of time, too—all that cyclicality also leads to shakeouts that the most competitive enterprises survive. These enterprises, thanks to their national scale and real competitive advantages, no longer depend on local-government funding and can now start to compete for the long term, both domestically and internationally.

That has certainly been the story in consumer electronics, where the top three players in personal computers control 50 percent of the domestic market, and in beer, where the top ten own 30 percent. It is starting to be the story in heavy industries, where companies such as China Qianjiang own 40 percent of the motorcycle market and Wanxiang dominates its niche in automotive components. Interestingly, it is not the foreign companies but the locals that tend to be the winners of the consolidation wars. The beer industry is a case in point: most foreign brewers, unprepared for tough domestic competition and rapid consolidation, entered and exited in the 1990s.

Moreover, I don't believe that FDI is linked to the development of China's capital markets or to a reform of the banking system. Multinationals account for only 15 percent of fixed-asset investment, so they don't drive the economy to a very great extent. China must rely on its own domestic financial resources to finance growth. As a result, the country's capital markets *are* being developed. And the government is fixing the banks through tough higher reserve margins, branch-level changes in performance management and incentives, and more flexible risk-based pricing.

As for the oft-stated view that China is trying to create global state-owned champions, it is at least partly a myth. The government does want to develop strong Chinese companies, but it does not expect them to be state enterprises, which are inefficient by definition. Indeed, it is now telling them that if they want to grow, they will have to get listed on the stock market. The government's policy for the first 20 years of its reform program was, "Let's do what's needed to establish markets." Its policy for the next 20 years will be,

"Let's get out of those markets." The global Chinese companies of tomorrow will be competitive, mostly listed, and entirely commercial in their aims and purposes.

Ultimately, you have to ask whether the inefficiencies of the Chinese approach outweigh what it has achieved for the economy overall. The answer, I think, is no. The government still controls most of the country's financial resources and has been reasonably good at allocating them—that's why the economy has grown so fast. Compared with the private sector in an efficient market, the government is no doubt worse at allocating funds. But China is not an efficient market, and the Indian model—essentially one with relatively little investment funding, whether by the government or the private sector—could not have achieved as much growth for the Chinese economy as the approach China's government actually took. The Indian model might not be adequate for India's economy either: the country's family-owned businesses and other private investors may be good at deciding what makes a sound investment for them, but they have not spent enough money to drive the kind of growth seen in China. It would not surprise me at all to see investment in India rise dramatically as foreign and domestic investors alike begin to recognize its potential going forward.

Sector by sector

Diana Farrell

The answer to the question, "Which is the better approach to economic development?" is not to be found at the national level. You have to look at what's going on in individual industries. And when you do, you find that supportive government policies that encourage competition drive good performance. Both China and India have some sluggish, inefficient industries that are heavily regulated and lack competitive dynamism. But both countries also have successful industries that thrive unfettered by poor regulation.

The McKinsey Global Institute has long argued that the key to high economic growth is productivity and that the main barrier to productivity gains is the raft of microlevel government regulations that hinder competition. This idea is well illustrated in the case of India.

At the high end of India's productivity spectrum is the information technology, software, and business-process-outsourcing sector. It's a big success story, having created hundreds of thousands of jobs and billions of dollars' worth of exports. As a new sector—and one whose potential the government, in my view, failed to recognize early on—it has avoided stifling regulation. IT, software, and outsourcing companies are exempt from the labor regulations that govern working hours and overtime in other sectors, and they have been allowed to receive FDI, which is prohibited in retailing, for example. Without this foreign money, it is debatable whether the sector could have taken off. By 2002 it already accounted for 15 percent of all foreign direct investment in India.

In the middle of the spectrum is the auto industry, which has seen dramatic change since the government began to liberalize it in the 1980s. By 1992 most of the barriers to foreign investment had been lifted, and this made it possible for output and labor productivity to soar. Prices have fallen and, even as the industry has consolidated, employment levels have held steady thanks to robust demand. Nonetheless, with tariffs on finished cars still relatively high, automakers remain sheltered from global competition and the sector is less efficient than it could be.

At the low end of the spectrum is the consumer electronics sector, which, despite the lifting of foreign-investment restrictions in the early 1990s, is still burdened by tariffs, taxes, and regulations. As a result,

Indian consumer electronics goods can't compete internationally and prices for local consumers are unnecessarily high. The performance of India's food-retailing industry is even worse. Partly as a result of a total ban on foreign investment, labor productivity is just 6 percent of US levels.

Now look at China, which also has some reasonably liberalized and highly competitive industries, including consumer electronics, in which labor productivity is double that of its Indian counterpart. Over the past 20 years, the industry has become globally competitive through a combination of FDI and intense competition among domestic companies. It is also remarkable for the relatively liberal approach the government has taken to regulation—probably because of a failure to see its growth potential. Today China makes $60 billion worth of consumer electronics goods a year.

The performance of China's auto industry—which was considered a strategic one and remains tightly regulated because of the government's desire to bring in technology and investment—is less clear-cut. The market has been opened up to foreign automakers, consumer demand has grown enormously, and prices have dropped. Yet the sector shows how government intervention can thwart the potential of foreign direct investment. Foreign automakers can invest only in joint ventures, they have to buy components from local suppliers, and tariffs shield the market from imports. Competition *is* beginning to increase as private companies grow stronger. But for the time being, the productivity of foreign joint ventures in China is low compared with that of plants in Japan or the United States— astounding given China's low labor costs.

Since there are such big differences in the performance of different sectors within the same country, it makes sense to compare the performance of India and China at the sector rather than the national level. In IT and business-process outsourcing, India is so far ahead of the game that China can't do anything during the next 10 or 15 years that would bring it close to catching up. In consumer electronics, however, China dominates, and India won't provide serious competition during the next ten years.

The auto sector is a toss-up. India's competitive forces have driven an enormous amount of innovation in the sector. Low-cost labor has been used instead of expensive automation, and local engineering talent has developed innovative new products such as the Scorpio—a sport utility vehicle that sells for a fraction of the price of an equivalent car in the United States. In China, large amounts of foreign direct investment have built a big industry, but regulation has so far limited its competitive potential.

It is far from clear which economy will emerge as the stronger one. The foundations of robust, sustainable economic growth must be built at the industry level, on the back of high productivity, which is achieved when governments ensure a level playing field through sound regulation and remove the barriers that stifle competition. Both China and India still have ample opportunity to help their industries and economies thrive.

Diana Farrell, Tarun Khanna, Jayant Sinha, and Jonathan R. Woetzel, *McKinsey Quarterly, 2004 Special Edition: China today.*

Note

1. The United Nations Conference on Trade and Development (UNC-TAD) database on foreign direct investment.

9

India: from emerging to surging

Amadeo M. Di Lodovico, William W. Lewis, Vincent Palmade, and Shirish Sankhe

IDEAS IN BRIEF

The three main barriers to faster growth in India are the multiplicity of regulations governing the product markets, distortions in the market for land, and widespread government ownership of businesses.

The rules and policies governing different sectors of India's economy impede GDP growth by 2.3 percent a year.

Close to 1.3 percent of lost growth a year results from distortions in the land market, distortions that have so far largely been ignored in the public debate.

Government-controlled entities account for around 43 percent of India's capital stock and 15 percent of employment outside agriculture. Their labor and capital productivity levels are well below those of their private competitors.

A decade ago, India and China had roughly the same gross domestic product per capita. But at $440, India's current GDP per capita is only about half of China's, and India's GDP is growing at a rate of only 6 percent a year, compared with China's 10 percent. That 6 percent is no mean feat, but could India grow faster?

Over the past 16 months, the McKinsey Global Institute (MGI) has studied the country's economy to see what is holding it back and which policy changes would accelerate its growth.[1] We studied 13 sectors in detail—two in agriculture, five in manufacturing, and six in services. Together, they account for 26 percent of India's GDP and 24 percent of its employment. (We also drew on similar MGI studies carried out in 12 other countries, including Brazil,[2] Poland,[3] Russia,[4] and South Korea.[5])

Our study found three main barriers to faster growth: the multiplicity of regulations governing product markets, distortions in the market for land, and widespread government ownership of businesses (see "What's slowing India's economic growth?"). We calculate that these three barriers together inhibit GDP growth by more than 4 percent a year. Removing them would free India's economy to grow as fast as China's, at 10 percent a year. Some 75 million new jobs would be created outside agriculture—enough not only to absorb the rapidly growing workforce but also to reabsorb the majority of workers displaced by productivity improvements.

Can these barriers be dismantled? We believe that they can if India's policymakers choose a deeper, faster process of reform than they have implemented so far.

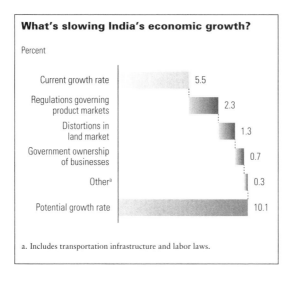

What's slowing India's economic growth?

Percent

Current growth rate	5.5
Regulations governing product markets	2.3
Distortions in land market	1.3
Government ownership of businesses	0.7
Other[a]	0.3
Potential growth rate	10.1

a. Includes transportation infrastructure and labor laws.

Barriers to productivity growth

Regulations governing product markets, land market distortions, and government-owned businesses—the three main barriers to India's economic growth—have their depressing effect largely because they protect most Indian companies from competition and thus from pressure to raise productivity. Countries with the highest productivity have the highest GDP per capita (see "Productivity paves the way") because the amount of goods and services each worker produces is the key determinant of a country's GDP per capita.

Product market barriers

Taken together, the rules and policies governing different sectors of the country's economy impede GDP growth by 2.3 percent a year. India's liberalized automotive industry shows what could be gained by removing these rules and policies. The Indian government, as part of its 1991 economic reforms, relaxed licensing

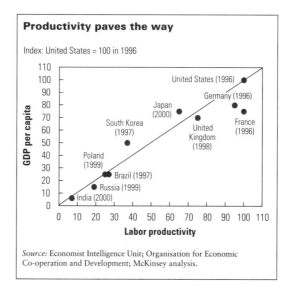

Productivity paves the way

Index: United States = 100 in 1996

Source: Economist Intelligence Unit; Organisation for Economic Co-operation and Development; McKinsey analysis.

requirements for carmakers and restrictions on foreign entrants into the industry. Competition increased dramatically, and the old, prereform automobile plants lost substantial market share. But demand for new, cheaper, and higher-quality Indian-made automobiles soared, so that employment in the industry rose by 11 percent from 1992–1993 to 1999–2000 despite productivity growth of no less than 256 percent during the same period.

India's current policy regime, at the sector level, has five features that are especially damaging to competition and therefore to the productivity of the country's industries.

Unfairness and ambiguity. Many policies restrict competition because they are inequitable and ill conceived. In telecommunications, for example, privately owned entrants must pay heavy fees for licenses to operate in prescribed areas, while government-owned incumbents pay no such fees and are at liberty to offer local-access and wireless services nationwide. Moreover, the rules concerning access to other operators' networks are unclear, and incumbents have used this ambiguity to delay the start of the privately owned entrants' operations. Indeed, these regulatory anomalies protect incumbents from competition by deterring some private telecoms from entering the market at all.

Uneven enforcement. The rules are not applied equally to all companies. Subscale steel mills, for example, frequently steal electricity and underreport their sales to avoid taxation. Larger, more visible players can't get away with such irregularities, so the less productive companies survive by competing unfairly (see "An unfair advantage").

Products reserved for small enterprises. Some 830 products are currently reserved for manufacture by firms below a certain size.

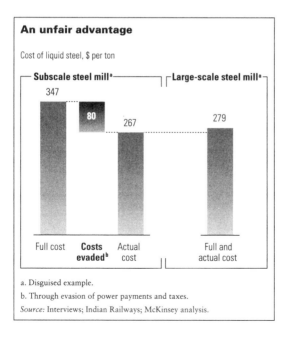

An unfair advantage

Cost of liquid steel, $ per ton

Subscale steel mill[a]   Large-scale steel mill[a]

347

80   267   279

Full cost   **Costs   Actual   Full and
            evaded[b]** cost   actual cost

a. Disguised example.
b. Through evasion of power payments and taxes.
Source: Interviews; Indian Railways; McKinsey analysis.

Producers of certain types of clothing and textiles, for instance, face limits on their spending for new plants—limits that protect clothing makers that are below efficient scale. As a result, typical Indian clothing plants have only about 50 machines, compared with more than 500 in a typical Chinese plant. Restrictions on imports of clothing from more productive countries protect the domestic markets of these subscale Indian players.

At present, moreover, their exports are protected too. Several countries, including the United States, import a guaranteed quota of Indian clothing each year. Not surprisingly, India's share of garment imports in countries without such quotas is much lower than it is in quota countries. As all such quotas are to be removed over the next five years, Indian exports will be highly vulnerable unless the sector can become more productive (see "Quota quandary: Export protection leaves sector vulnerable").

Restrictions on foreign direct investment. Certain sectors of the Indian economy—retailing, for example—cannot receive for-

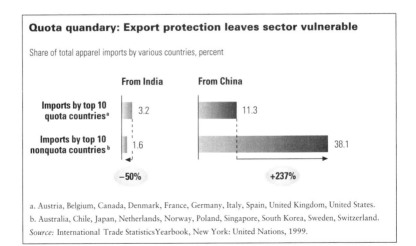

Quota quandary: Export protection leaves sector vulnerable

Share of total apparel imports by various countries, percent

	From India	From China
Imports by top 10 quota countries[a]	3.2	11.3
Imports by top 10 nonquota countries[b]	1.6	38.1
	−50%	+237%

a. Austria, Belgium, Canada, Denmark, France, Germany, Italy, Spain, United Kingdom, United States.
b. Australia, Chile, Japan, Netherlands, Norway, Poland, Singapore, South Korea, Sweden, Switzerland.
Source: International Trade Statistics Yearbook, New York: United Nations, 1999.

eign direct investment (FDI), and this prohibition closes off a fruitful source of technology and skills. Best-practice global retailers, whose international experience helps them to build operations quickly by tailoring their formats to local environments, have enabled the retail sectors in Brazil, China, Poland, and Thailand to develop rapidly. Foreign retailers also prompt local supply chains to improve by stimulating investment and productivity growth in food processing and wholesaling, for example. Together with land market reforms (discussed later), allowing FDI in food retailing would make it possible for India's supermarkets to increase their market share to 25 percent nationwide in ten years, from 2 percent currently, and to offer prices that would on average be 9 percent lower than those of local grocery stores. Indian standards of living across the social spectrum would rise immediately.

Licensing or quasi-licensing. In several sectors of the Indian economy—the dairy industry, to give one example—operators need a license from the government to compete. Although the licensing of dairy processors was supposed to ensure high levels of quality and hygiene, the licensing authority has in fact prevented high-quality private dairy plants from competing in certain areas, thus protecting government-owned plants and cooperative dairies from competition and from any incentive to shed excess labor or improve operations. Removing these restrictions would increase competition among processors, forcing them to make improvements by, for instance, using chilling centers and working with farmers to improve cattle breeds and milk yields (see "Milking the benefits of competition.")

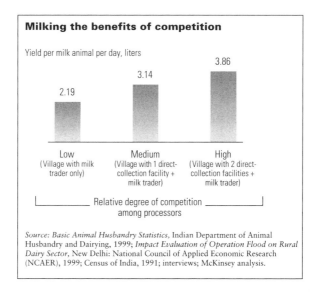

Milking the benefits of competition

Yield per milk animal per day, liters

		3.86
	3.14	
2.19		

Low
(Village with milk trader only)

Medium
(Village with 1 direct-collection facility + milk trader)

High
(Village with 2 direct-collection facilities + milk trader)

Relative degree of competition among processors

Source: *Basic Animal Husbandry Statistics*, Indian Department of Animal Husbandry and Dairying, 1999; *Impact Evaluation of Operation Flood on Rural Dairy Sector*, New Delhi: National Council of Applied Economic Research (NCAER), 1999; Census of India, 1991; interviews; McKinsey analysis.

Distortions in the land market

Close to 1.3 percent of lost growth a year, our calculations suggest, results from distortions in the land market—distortions that have so far largely been ignored in the public debate. These distortions limit the land available for housing and retailing, which are the largest domestic sectors outside agriculture. Less room to expand in these sectors means less competition among housing developers and retailers. Scarcity has helped make Indian land prices the highest among all Asian nations relative to average incomes (see "Outlandish: High costs relative to income"). Three distortions in the land market are especially significant.

Unclear ownership. Title to most land parcels in India—90 percent by one estimate—is unclear, and the problem might take Indian courts a century to resolve at their current rate of progress. This lack of clarity about who owns what makes it immensely

Outlandish: High costs relative to income

Ratio of cost of land per square meter to GDP per capita in 1999;
index: New Delhi = 100

Mumbai	115
New Delhi	100
Bangalore	52
Taipei	22
Seoul	13
Jakarta	13
Singapore	12
Tokyo	9
Bangkok	7
Sydney	6
Kuala Lumpur	2

Source: *Asia Pacific Property Trends*, Colliers Jardine Pacific, October 1999.

difficult to buy land for retail and housing development. Property developers and individual landowners also have trouble raising financing, since they can't offer as collateral for loans any land to which they don't have clear title. Not surprisingly, most new housing developments are constructed on land already owned by the developers or the few insiders who know how to speed up the bureaucratic title-clearing process. Streamlining this process and revising the laws on land ownership would boost competition in construction. Competitive builders would improve their productivity and offer houses at lower prices. The sluggish Indian construction market would expand dramatically.

Counterproductive taxation. Low property taxes, ineffective tax collection, and subsidized user charges for power and water leave local governments unable to recover the cost of their investments in infrastructure, particularly in suburban areas. In Delhi, for example, water is supplied at only 10 percent of its true cost. Property taxes collected in Mumbai (formerly Bombay) amount to only 0.002 percent of the buildings' estimated capital value; the usual ratio in developed countries is 1 to 2 percent. With more efficient collection of higher taxes, local governments could invest in the infrastructure to support new housing developments on more and larger parcels of suburban land. Customers would have more choices, and developers would have to compete harder. Further, if developers could build up to 25 houses in a project instead of the single homes they more typically construct today, building costs would fall by up to 25 percent.

Conversely, stamp duties[6] are extraordinarily high in India: close to 8 to 10 percent of the value of the property changing hands. Not surprisingly, this expense discourages the registration of land and real-estate transactions.

Inflexible zoning, rent, and tenancy laws. Land in city centers that would otherwise be available for new retail outlets and apartments is "frozen" by protected tenancies, rent controls, and zoning laws. Protected tenants cannot be evicted and will never voluntarily surrender their cheap tenancies, so their ancient buildings can never be sold or rebuilt. Tenancy laws also restrict competition: subsidized rents, for example, allow traditional inner-city counter stores to persist in their operational inefficiencies. But in Chennai (formerly Madras), the capital of India's southern state of Tamil Nadu, where rent control and zoning laws are less stringent, modern supermarkets already account for almost 20 percent of total food retailing compared with less than 1 percent in cities that have higher average incomes, such as Mumbai and Delhi.

Government ownership of businesses

Government-controlled entities still account for around 43 percent of India's capital stock and 15 percent of employment outside agriculture. Their labor and capital productivity levels are well below those of their private competitors (see "Government ownership hinders productivity"), since public-sector managers experience little performance pressure. The near-monopoly status of government-owned companies in sectors such as oil, power, and telecommunications, for example, ensures that such companies

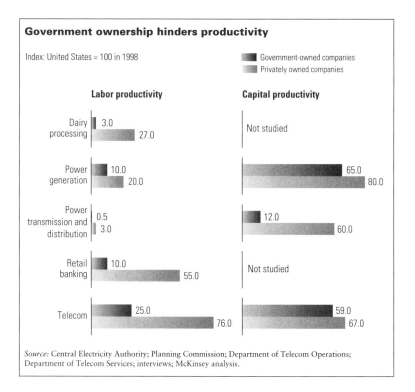

Government ownership hinders productivity

Index: United States = 100 in 1998

- ■ Government-owned companies
- ▨ Privately owned companies

Labor productivity

Dairy processing	3.0 / 27.0
Power generation	10.0 / 20.0
Power transmission and distribution	0.5 / 3.0
Retail banking	10.0 / 55.0
Telecom	25.0 / 76.0

Capital productivity

Dairy processing	Not studied
Power generation	65.0 / 80.0
Power transmission and distribution	12.0 / 60.0
Retail banking	Not studied
Telecom	59.0 / 67.0

Source: Central Electricity Authority; Planning Commission; Department of Telecom Operations; Department of Telecom Services; interviews; McKinsey analysis.

will be profitable however unproductive they may be. Failing state-owned companies in industries open to competition, such as steel and retail banking, can get government support, so that they too manage to survive despite their inefficiency. In electric power and telecommunications, the government controls both the large players and the regulators, thus creating an uneven playing field for private competitors.

India's electricity sector illustrates how government control of companies can promote inefficiency. Government-owned state electricity boards lose a staggering 30 to 40 percent of their power, mostly to theft. By comparison, best-practice private power distributors lose only around 10 percent, mostly for technical reasons. Government subsidies, and corruption, give public-sector managers less motivation to control theft. Subsidies also limit their incentive to prevent blackouts and to maintain power lines—tasks that private companies undertake with better results. Privatizing the state electricity boards would save their government subsidies, amounting to almost 1.5 percent of GDP, and oblige managers to improve their financial and thus their operational performance. These managers would have to monitor theft and improve the capital and labor productivity of the facilities.

Dismantling the barriers

Thirteen policy changes would dismantle most of these critical barriers to higher productivity and growth (*see* "How to make India's economy grow"). The changes include eliminating the practice of reserving products for small-scale manufacturers, rationalizing taxes and excise duties, establishing effective and procompetitive regulation as well as powerful independent regulators, reducing import duties, removing restrictions on foreign investment, reforming property and tenancy laws, and under-taking widespread privatization. If the government carried out these changes over the next two to three years, we believe that the economy would achieve most of the projected 10 percent yearly growth by 2005.

Such profound changes would certainly prompt resistance in the name of social objectives, especially from those protected by the current regulatory regime. But the fact is that the current policies have not achieved their social purposes, however wor-thy: many have been counterproductive. Reserving products for small companies, for example, has cost India manufacturing jobs by preventing companies from becoming productive enough to compete in export markets. Similarly, tenancy laws designed to protect tenants have driven up nonprotected rents and real-estate prices, thus making ordinary decent housing unaffordable to many Indians.

Critics might still argue that the increase in GDP resulting from these policy changes will all flow to the already rich. But after carefully examining the expected effects of the proposed reforms on the Indian economy, we can see that, once again, the opposite is true. By creating a virtuous cycle of broad-based growth in GDP, the changes will benefit every Indian. For example, the real incomes of farming families—the poorest group—will rise by at least 40 percent over ten years.

The effects of reform

India's economy has three types of sectors. Modern ones, with pro-duction processes resembling those in modern economies, provide 24 percent of employment and 47 percent of output. Transi-tional sectors provide 16 percent of employment and 27 percent of output. Agricultural sectors provide 60 percent of employment and 26 percent of output. The transitional sectors include those responsible for the informal goods and services consumed by a growing urban population: street vending, domestic service, small-scale food processing, and cheap mud housing, for example. Transitional businesses typically require elementary skills and very little capital and therefore tend to absorb workers moving out of agriculture.

What will happen to the economy if India immediately dismantles all existing barriers to higher productivity? Our analysis shows that the resulting increase in labor and capital productivity will boost growth in the overall GDP to 10 percent a year, release investment capital worth 5.7 percent of GDP, and generate 75 million new jobs outside agriculture, in both the modern and the transitional sectors.

Labor productivity

Eliminating all the productivity barriers would almost double India's rate of growth in labor productivity, to almost 8 percent a year, over the next ten years. The modern sectors would account for around 90 percent of the growth (see "A more productive future for India?"), which would remain low in the other two sectors. There may be small improvements in agricultural productivity, mainly from yield increases. But the massive improvement in agricultural productivity that mechanized farming has supported in developed countries isn't likely to occur in India for at least ten years while there is still a surplus of low-cost rural labor to deter farmers from investing in advanced machines. In the transitional sectors, enterprises have inherently low labor productivity because they use labor-intensive low-tech materi-

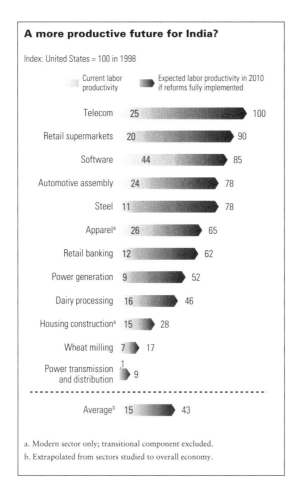

A more productive future for India?

Index: United States = 100 in 1998

Current labor productivity

Expected labor productivity in 2010 if reforms fully implemented

Telecom	25	100
Retail supermarkets	20	90
Software	44	85
Automotive assembly	24	78
Steel	11	78
Apparel[a]	26	65
Retail banking	12	62
Power generation	9	52
Dairy processing	16	46
Housing construction[a]	15	28
Wheat milling	7	17
Power transmission and distribution	1	9
Average[b]	15	43

a. Modern sector only; transitional component excluded.
b. Extrapolated from sectors studied to overall economy.

als, technologies, or business formats. So although these sectors will grow to meet rising demand, their labor productivity will stay about the same.

Capital productivity

If all the barriers were removed, capital productivity in the modern sectors would grow by at least 50 percent over the next three to four years. Increased competition would force managers to eliminate the tremendous time and cost overruns of capital projects and the low utilization of installed capacity—problems that managers can get away with now, especially in state-run enterprises. If equitably enforced, regulation to ensure healthy competition would prevent the unwise investments that are common today, such as the construction of subscale and under-utilized steel mills.

Investment

Many policymakers and commentators believe that it would take a level of investment equal to more than 35 percent of India's GDP—an almost unattainable amount—to make the country's GDP grow by 10 percent a year. But our analyses suggest that by eliminating barriers to higher productivity, India can achieve this rate of GDP growth with a level of investment equivalent to only 30 percent of GDP a year for a decade, less than China invested from 1988 to 1998. Although still a challenge, this 30 percent rate is certainly achievable, since removing the barriers to productivity will unleash for investment extra funds equivalent to the consequent drop in the public deficit and encourage greater foreign direct investment. These sources, by themselves, would be sufficient to increase investment to 30.2 percent of GDP, from its current level of 24.5 percent.

How would the funds be released? Removing the barriers to higher productivity would, first, generate extra revenue for the government through more efficient taxation—particularly on property—and from privatization. Second, reform would save what the government now spends on subsidies for unprofitable state-owned enterprises. As a result, the government's budget deficit would decrease by at least 4 percent of GDP, which would then become available for private investment elsewhere.

Current flows of FDI into India are worth just 0.5 percent of

GDP. Many developing countries, including China, Malaysia, Poland, and Thailand, consistently attract foreign direct investment worth more than 3 percent of their annual GDP. We estimate that removing the three major barriers by opening all modern sectors of India's economy to well-regulated competition and lifting restrictions on foreign direct investment will increase it by at least 1.7 percent of GDP within three years.

Employment

Productivity growth and increased investment will create more than 75 million new jobs outside agriculture, compared with the 24 million projected as a result of current policies. Employment in the modern sectors will increase by around 32 million jobs as higher productivity and lower prices stimulate demand. Similarly, employment in India's transitional sectors will grow by around 43 million jobs. The transitional sectors—often overlooked by policymakers—will play a crucial role in India's evolution from an agricultural to a more modern economy, since it is these sectors that will initially absorb workers moving out of agriculture. Agricultural wages will therefore rise.

This migration of labor among sectors is a feature of all strongly growing economies, for though higher productivity displaces labor in some sectors, it stimulates higher overall employment. But what of the workers laid off by overstaffed companies in newly productive modern sectors? Most of these people will be able to find work in efficient companies in their own or other growing sectors. Many overstaffed companies, such as small steel plants, state electricity boards, and branches of government-owned banks, are located near towns or cities, where most of the new jobs are likely to emerge. Redundant workers close to retirement age will be able to take up early retirement packages, which in India are generally worth three to four years' salary.

India will be a very different country in ten years, with a GDP of around $1.1 trillion, if these reforms are undertaken. Average individual Indians will be more than twice as rich and will probably live in the world's fastest-growing economy. Best of all, this is no pipe dream but an achievable goal—if the government and the people of India act decisively and soon.

How to make India's economy grow

Category	Action		Key sectors directly affected
Product market	1	Completely eliminate the reservation of products for small-scale industry; start with 68 sectors accounting for 80 percent of output of reserved sectors	• 836 manufactured goods
	2	Equalize sales taxes and excise dutles for all categories of players in each sector and strengthen enforcement	• Hotels and restaurants • Manufacturing (such as apparel, steel, and textiles) • Retail trade
	3	Establish an effective regulatory framework and strong regulatory bodies	• Power • Telecom • Water supply
	4	Remove all licensing and quasi-licensing restrictions that limit the number of players in affected Industries	• Banking • Dairy processing • Petroleum marketing • Provident-fund management • Sugar
	5	Reduce import dutles on all goods to the levels of Southeast Asian countries (10 percent) over five years	• Manufacturing

Category		Action	Key sectors directly affected
Product market	6	Remove the ban on foreign direct investment in the retail sector and allow unrestricted foreign direct investment in all sectors	• Insurance • Retail trade • Telecom
Land market	7	Resolve unclear real-estate titles by setting up fast-track courts to settle disputes, computerizing land records, freeing all property from constraints on sale, and removing limits on property ownership	• Construction • Hotels and restaurants • Retail trade
	8	Raise property taxes and user charges for municipal services and cut stamp duties (tax on property transactions) to promote the development of residential and commercial land and to increase the land market's liquidity	
	9	Reform tenancy laws to allow rents to move to market levels	
Government ownership	10	Privatize the electricity sector and all companies owned by the central and state governments; in the electricity sector, start by privatizing distribution; in all other sectors, first privatize the largest companies	• Airlines • Banking and insurance • Manufacturing and mining • Power • Telecommunications
Others	11	Reform labor laws by repealing section 5-B of the Industrial Disputes Act, by introducing standard retrenchment-compensation norms and by allowing full flexibility in the use of contract labor	• Labor-intensive manufacturing and service sectors
	12	Transfer the management of the existing transport infrastructure to the private sector; contract out the construction and management of new infrastructure to it	• Airports • Ports • Roads
	13	Strengthen extension services to help farmers improve their yields	• Agriculture

Amadeo M. Di Lodovico, William W. Lewis, Vincent Palmade, and Shirish Sankhe, *McKinsey Quarterly, 2001 Special Edition: Emerging markets.*

Notes

1. The study was conducted by the authors as well as by the following McKinsey consultants: Neeraj Agrawal (Delhi), Angelique Augereau (MGI), Vivake Bhalla (London), Axel Flasbarth (Berlin), Chandrika Gadi (Delhi), Deepak Goyal (Delhi), Jayant Kulkarni (Dallas), Anish Tawakley (Mumbai), Catherine Thomas (an alumnus of the firm), Sanoke Viswanathan (Mumbai), and Alkesh Wadhwani (Mumbai). The full report is available on-line at www.mckinsey.com.

2. See Martin N. Baily, Heinz-Peter Elstrodt, William Bebb Jones Jr., William W. Lewis, Vincent Palmade, Norbert Sack, and Eric W. Zitzewitz, "Will Brazil seize its future?" *The McKinsey Quarterly,* 1998 Number 3, pp. 74–91.

3. See Amadeo M. Di Lodovico, Axel Flasbarth, Björn Klocke, William W. Lewis, Vincent Palmade, and Catherine Thomas, "Sustaining Poland's hard-won prosperity," *The McKinsey Quarterly,* 2000 Number 2, special edition: Europe in transition, pp. 88–97.

4. See Alexei Beltyukov, M. James Kondo, William W. Lewis, Michael M. Obermayer, Vincent Palmade, and Alex Reznikovitch, "Reflections on Russia," *The McKinsey Quarterly,* 2000 Number 1, pp. 19–41.

5. See Martin N. Baily, Cuong V. Do, Yong Sung Kim, William W. Lewis, Victoria Lee Nam, Vincent Palmade, and Eric W. Zitzewitz, "The roots of Korea's crisis," *The McKinsey Quarterly,* 1998 Number 2, pp. 76–83.

6. A tax levied on property transactions.

10

A richer future for India

Diana Farrell and Adil S. Zainulbhai

IDEAS IN BRIEF

The introduction of foreign competition in IT, business-process outsourcing, and the automotive industry has prompted Indian companies to revamp their operations and boost productivity, and some have become formidable global competitors.

India's competitive intensity could give it a better position than China to serve as a global, low-cost, auto-manufacturing base.

To attract foreign investment in labor-intensive industries, the government should consider making labor laws more flexible.

ndian voters sent a clear message in the 2004 elections about the need for broad-based economic growth that lifts all boats. But some members of the winning coalition may well misinterpret that message. India's recent experience—and that of its Asian neighbors—shows that continuing rural poverty stems not from too much economic reform but rather from too little. Since liberalization began, in 1991, annual GDP growth has been twice as high as it had been previously. As a result, poverty rates have fallen by nearly a third in both rural and urban areas. The celebrated software and outsourcing industries are only the latest evidence of the effectiveness of the reforms, which have created hundreds of thousands of high-paying jobs and generated billions in export revenues.

The challenge facing the ruling coalition is to extend the success of the IT and outsourcing industries into the broader economy. To that end, foreign investment and global competition must be allowed to reach more sectors, including some in which the government now plays a significant role. Although India has broadly cut import duties and increased foreign-ownership limits over the past ten years, large parts of the economy remain sheltered by high tariffs and restrictions on foreign direct investment (see "A half-closed door"), which amounts to just 0.7 percent of India's GDP, compared with 4.2 percent in China and 3.2 percent in Brazil. Imports total less than $70 billion—a small fraction of China's $413 billion.

Research by the McKinsey Global Institute[1] indicates that the foreign direct investment (FDI) that *did* find its way to India has had an overwhelmingly positive impact. The introduction of

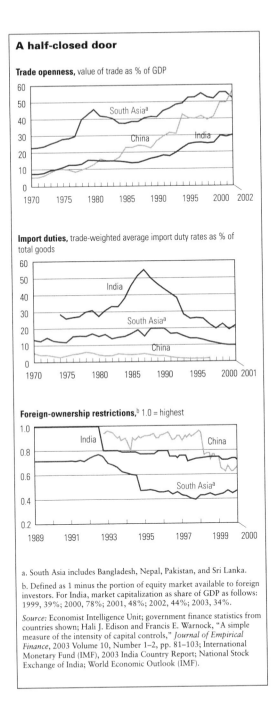

A half-closed door

Trade openness, value of trade as % of GDP

South Asia[a]

China   India

Import duties, trade-weighted average import duty rates as % of total goods

India

South Asia[a]

China

Foreign-ownership restrictions,[b] 1.0 = highest

India   China

South Asia[a]

a. South Asia includes Bangladesh, Nepal, Pakistan, and Sri Lanka.

b. Defined as 1 minus the portion of equity market available to foreign investors. For India, market capitalization as share of GDP as follows: 1999, 39%; 2000, 78%; 2001, 48%; 2002, 44%; 2003, 34%.

Source: Economist Intelligence Unit; government finance statistics from countries shown; Hali J. Edison and Francis E. Warnock, "A simple measure of the intensity of capital controls," *Journal of Empirical Finance,* 2003 Volume 10, Number 1–2, pp. 81–103; International Monetary Fund (IMF), 2003 India Country Report; National Stock Exchange of India; World Economic Outlook (IMF).

foreign competition in IT, business-process outsourcing, and the automotive industry has prompted Indian companies to revamp their operations and boost productivity, and some have become formidable global competitors. Thousands of new jobs have been created in these industries. Consumers benefit from lower prices, better quality, and a wider selection of products and services, while domestic demand has soared in response to lower prices.

The task now is to build on the current momentum by replicating these successes across the economy. Earlier MGI research[2] found that product market regulations, the lack of clear land titles, and pervasive government ownership were preventing India from achieving 10 percent annual GDP growth. MGI's latest research shows that the country must go further in lowering trade and foreign-investment barriers if it is to continue integrating itself into the global economy.

Shining stars

India's $1.5 billion outsourcing business illustrates how foreign investment and trade have benefited the country. Along with IT and software, business-process outsourcing is perhaps the most open sector. In 2002, it attracted 15 percent of total FDI and accounted for 10 percent of all exports. By 2008, it is expected to attract one-third of all FDI and to generate $60 billion a year in exports, creating nearly a million new jobs in the process.

Without early investments by multinational companies, the outsourcing industry probably would never have emerged (see "Offshoring takes off"). Pioneers such as British Airways and GE were among the first to see the opportunity to move IT and other back-office operations to India. The success of these com-

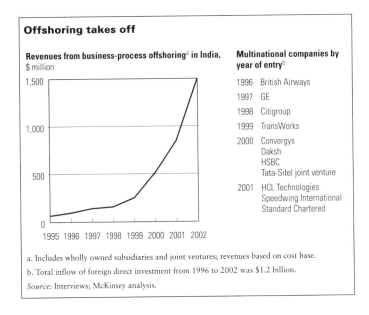

Offshoring takes off

Revenues from business-process offshoring[a] in India,
$ million

Multinational companies by
year of entry[b]

1996	British Airways
1997	GE
1998	Citigroup
1999	TransWorks
2000	Convergys Daksh HSBC Tata-Sitel joint venture
2001	HCL Technologies Speedwing International Standard Chartered

a. Includes wholly owned subsidiaries and joint ventures; revenues based on cost base.
b. Total inflow of foreign direct investment from 1996 to 2002 was $1.2 billion.
Source: Interviews; McKinsey analysis.

panies demonstrated to the world that the country was a credible offshoring destination. The multinationals trained thousands of local workers, many of whom transferred their skills to Indian companies that sprang up in response. Although Indian outsourcing firms now control over half of the intensely competitive global IT and back-office outsourcing market, all of the leading ones started as joint ventures or subsidiaries of multinational companies or were founded by managers who had worked for them.

Of course, allowing foreign investment in an industry that has no large Indian companies was relatively painless. It is far harder to put local incumbents in the line of fire. Yet India has done so in its automotive industry, with impressive results. Until 1983, high tariffs and a ban on foreign investment shielded government-owned automakers, such as Premier Automobiles Limited (PAL), from global competition. Local incumbents produced just two car models, both based on antiquated technology, between them, and charged high prices. In 1983, Suzuki Motor was allowed to take a minority stake in a joint venture with Maruti Udyog, another government-owned enterprise, to produce passenger cars. The new competition forced the incumbents to respond. Within a few years, eight Indian car models were in production, and all of them—including those from PAL—were of better quality than the cars produced before this liberation took place.

In 1992, the government lifted many of the remaining barriers to foreign investment in the auto industry. Nine additional foreign carmakers responded, and today competition is stiff. As a result, labor productivity has increased more than threefold, in part because PAL has been forced out of business. Prices have fallen steadily by 8 to 10 percent annually in all market segments, unleashing a burst of consumer demand. Despite higher productivity and the closure of PAL, employment has held steady and workers have benefited from higher wages.

As of 2004, India's $5 billion auto industry has been expanding by 15 percent a year—one of the world's fastest automotive-industry growth rates—and produces 13 times more cars than it did in 1983. This year, in view of the greater competitive intensity in the market, India may be better positioned than China is to become a global low-cost auto-manufacturing base. None of this would have been possible had India's carmakers remained isolated from the world.

Hiding behind trade barriers

The dynamic growth and competitiveness of India's outsourcing and automotive industries stand in contrast to most of its economy, where continuing restrictions on foreign investment and trade dampen competition and help inefficient companies survive.

Another sector, food retailing, illustrates how Indian industry fares when foreign investment is banned entirely. Labor productivity, for instance, is a mere 5 percent of US levels, in part because street markets and mom-and-pop counter stores account for 98 percent of the market, modern store formats (like supermarkets and hypermarkets) for just 2 percent. But productivity averages just 20 percent of US levels even in Indian supermarkets as a result of their small scale, poor merchandising and marketing skills, and inefficient operations. In other emerging markets, including Brazil, China, and Mexico, global retailers such as Carrefour and Wal-Mart Stores have intensified competition and increased productivity. If these retailers could invest in India, improved Indian supermarkets could, we estimate, offer prices 10 percent lower than those of traditional grocery stores. Indian consumers across the social spectrum would benefit, and as many as eight million new jobs would be created.

Getting the full benefit of foreign investment calls for competition within industries, since it forces companies to improve their operations and innovate. Many forms of protection and regulation can stifle competition and thus limit the impact of foreign investment. The consumer electronics industry is a prime example. The government lifted foreign-investment restrictions in the sector in the early 1990s. From 1996 to 2001, FDI in it averaged $300 million annually—20 percent of the total for India—a large sum, although just 8 percent of the consumer electronics investment going to China and just half of the investment going to Brazil and Mexico. Still, the entry of multinational players has boosted the local industry's productivity and given Indian consumers more choice and lower prices.

Despite these gains, consumer electronics goods made in India still can't compete internationally, and the country's consumers pay unduly high prices for them. The industry's average labor productivity is only half of Chinese and 13 percent of South Korean levels. Tariffs, taxes, and regulations are the main culprits. Tariffs of 35 to 40 percent on finished goods keep out imports and allow inefficient companies to continue operating. They also force even the best manufacturers to operate with subscale plants when, as usually happens, Indian demand doesn't justify larger scale. Tariffs on inputs and indirect taxes (mostly sales and value-added taxes) add substantially to the price of final goods, further limiting demand (see "A raw deal for India"). Meanwhile, labor laws that prevent the rationalization of plants and limit the use of contract labor increase production costs for both foreign and domestic companies. Red tape in getting export licenses and inefficiencies in India's ports make exporting finished goods prohibitively expensive (see "Ports of crawl").

These same problems limit foreign investment and prevent many industries—including banking, heavy industry, and textiles— from reaching their full potential. Ultimately, consumers and workers pay through higher prices and the anemic pace of job creation.

Going global

India has clearly benefited from closer integration into the global economy in industries such as automotive, business-process outsourcing, and IT. To build on that success, the government must now lower trade and foreign-investment barriers still further.

First, tariff levels should be cut to an average of 10 percent, matching those of India's neighbors in the Association of South East Asian Nations (ASEAN). Although progress has been made on tariffs, the Indian government still prohibits imports of many

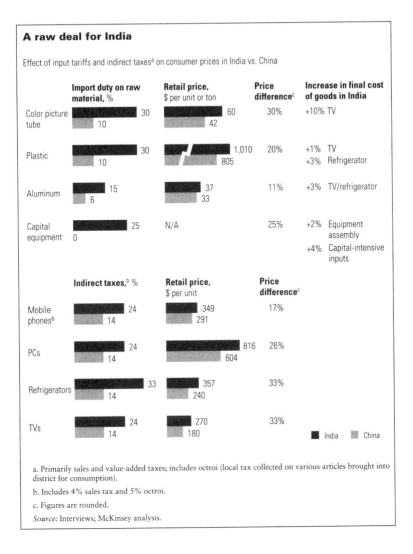

A raw deal for India

Effect of input tariffs and indirect taxes[a] on consumer prices in India vs. China

	Import duty on raw material, %	Retail price, $ per unit or ton	Price difference[c]	Increase in final cost of goods in India	
Color picture tube	30 / 10	60 / 42	30%	+10%	TV
Plastic	30 / 10	1,010 / 805	20%	+1% / +3%	TV / Refrigerator
Aluminum	15 / 6	37 / 33	11%	+3%	TV/refrigerator
Capital equipment	25 / 0	N/A	25%	+2% / +4%	Equipment assembly / Capital-intensive inputs

	Indirect taxes,[b] %	Retail price, $ per unit	Price difference[c]
Mobile phones[b]	24 / 14	349 / 291	17%
PCs	24 / 14	816 / 604	26%
Refrigerators	33 / 14	357 / 240	33%
TVs	24 / 14	270 / 180	33%

■ India ■ China

a. Primarily sales and value-added taxes; includes octroi (local tax collected on various articles brought into district for consumption).
b. Includes 4% sales tax and 5% octroi.
c. Figures are rounded.
Source: Interviews; McKinsey analysis.

goods and protects inefficient companies from foreign competition. To give those companies a chance to improve their operations, the government might first lower duties on capital goods and inputs. Then, over several years, it could reduce them on finished goods.

Foreign-ownership restrictions should be lifted throughout the economy as well, except in strategic areas, notably defense. At present, foreign ownership is not only prohibited altogether in

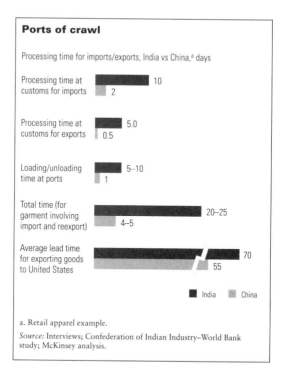

Ports of crawl

Processing time for imports/exports, India vs China,[a] days

Processing time at customs for imports
India: 10
China: 2

Processing time at customs for exports
India: 5.0
China: 0.5

Loading/unloading time at ports
India: 5–10
China: 1

Total time (for garment involving import and reexport)
India: 20–25
China: 4–5

Average lead time for exporting goods to United States
India: 70
China: 55

■ India   ▨ China

a. Retail apparel example.

Source: Interviews; Confederation of Indian Industry–World Bank study; McKinsey analysis.

industries such as agriculture, real estate, and retailing but also limited to minority stakes in many others, such as banking, insurance, and telecommunications.

India's government should also reconsider the expensive but often ineffective incentives it offers foreign companies to attract foreign investment, for these resources would be put to better use improving the country's roads, telecom infrastructure, power supply, and logistics. What's more, MGI research found that the government often gives away substantial sums of money for investments that would have been made anyway.[3] (To give one example, it has waived the 35 percent tax on corporate profits for foreign companies that move business-process operations to India, even though the country dominates the global industry.) Moreover, state governments often conduct unproductive bidding wars with one another and give away an assortment of tax holidays, import duty exemptions, and subsidized land and power.

Yet MGI surveys show that foreign executives place relatively little value on these incentives and would rather see the government invest resources in the country's poor infrastructure.

Finally, interviews with foreign executives showed us that India's labor laws deter foreign investment in some industries. It is no coincidence that software and business-outsourcing companies are exempt from many labor regulations, such as those regarding hours and overtime. Executives tell us that without these exemptions, it would be impossible to perform back-office operations in India. To attract foreign investment in labor-intensive industries, the government should therefore consider making labor laws more flexible.

Some Indian policymakers might argue that the reforms proposed here would undermine long-held social objectives, such as creating employment. But the evidence shows that regulations on foreign investment, foreign trade, and labor have actually slowed economic growth and lowered the standard of living. A decade ago, India's per capita income was nearly the same as China's; today, China's is almost twice as high.

India's economy has made real progress, but further liberalization will be needed to sustain its growth. The country now has 40 million people looking for work, and an additional 35 million will join the labor force over the next three years. Creating jobs for all these Indians will require more dynamic and competitive industries across the economy. Opening up to foreign competition, not hiding from it, is the answer.

Diana Farrell and Adil S. Zainulbhai,
McKinsey Quarterly, 2004 Special Edition: What global executives think.

Notes

1. The full report, *New Horizons: Multinational Company Investment in Developing Economies,* October 2003, is available free of charge at www.mckinsey.com/knowledge/mgi/newhorizons.

2. Amadeo M. Di Lodovico, William W. Lewis, Vincent Palmade, and Shirish Sankhe, "India—From emerging to surging," *The McKinsey Quarterly,* 2001 special edition: Emerging markets, pp. 28–50 (www.mckinseyquarterly.com/links/13271).

3. Diana Farrell, Jaana K. Remes, and Heiner Schulz, "The truth about foreign direct investment in emerging markets," *The McKinsey Quarterly,* 2004 Number 1, pp. 24–35 (www.mckinseyquarterly.com/links/13273).

11

How Brazil can grow

Heinz-Peter Elstrodt, Jorge A. Fergie, and
Martha Laboissière

IDEAS IN BRIEF

The five main barriers to Brazil's growth are a very large informal
economy, macroeconomic factors that hinder investment,
inappropriate regulations, poor public services, and weak
infrastructure.

The chief culprit for Brazil's underperformance has been its
failure to boost growth in labor productivity—the primary
determinant of a nation's GDP per capita.

Two-thirds of Brazil's productivity deficit can be tackled by
changes in government policy. The rest will come when the
economy moves onto a sustainable, healthy growth track.

Brazil's immense economic potential is undisputed. Expectations run high within and beyond its borders that the country could be the next emerging economy, after China and India, to see GDP growth take off.[1] It has good universities, a huge domestic market, and copious natural resources. Yet according to the International Monetary Fund, Brazil's GDP per capita has grown by an annual average of only 1.5 percent over the past ten years. This is one of the lowest growth figures of all the countries monitored by the Fund, and particularly low for a developing nation.

Hyperinflation, the economy's most pressing problem at the end of the past decade, is no longer a specter. Brazil's current fiscal and monetary policies have drawn praise for their role in stabilizing the macroeconomic framework.[2] Indeed some sectors of the economy, particularly retail banking, telecom and export agriculture, are flourishing. The problem is that these sectors employ only a tiny fraction of the workforce. Most people are employed in sectors that have very low productivity growth, particularly retail, residential construction and farming for the domestic market.

For the mass of Brazilians trying to make a living, life has not become noticeably easier as inflation has subsided. Low GDP growth means their per capita incomes are falling behind relative to those in other developing countries. In 1995 Brazil's per capita GDP was 46 percent of the Korean level: now it is only 39 percent.

McKinsey's São Paulo office, in collaboration with the McKinsey Global Institute, has examined Brazil's economy to find out just how far its productivity is falling behind, and what stops it from improving. The five main barriers we identified look formidable: a very large informal economy, macroeconomic factors that hinder investment, inappropriate regulations, poor public services, and weak infrastructure. The good news, however, is that all of them can be tackled with the right policies. Indeed, other countries, such as Spain and Ireland, have adjusted their economic policies to address similar problems and have succeeded. Brazilians should take hope.

Brazil's productivity problem

Building on a previous analysis conducted in 1998[3] and similar MGI studies undertaken in another 16 countries, we compared the performance of Brazil's economy with that of the United States in eight sectors—agriculture, automotive, food retailing, government, home construction, retail banking, steel, and telecommunications. Together, these sectors account for 37 percent of Brazilian employment and 46 percent of the country's GDP.

The new analysis makes clear that the chief culprit for Brazil's underperformance has been its failure to boost growth in labor productivity—the primary determinant of a nation's GDP per capita. Between 1995 and 2005, Brazil's productivity grew by only 0.3 percent a year—compared with 2.8 percent in the United States, 8.4 percent in China, and the 3.5 percent achieved by neighboring Chile. Brazil's labor productivity gap with the United States rose from 77 to 82 percentage points during this decade (see "Brazilian labor productivity performance").

Our examination revealed that around one-third of the difference in productivity between the United States and Brazil is due to factors that are inherent in Brazil's position in the economic

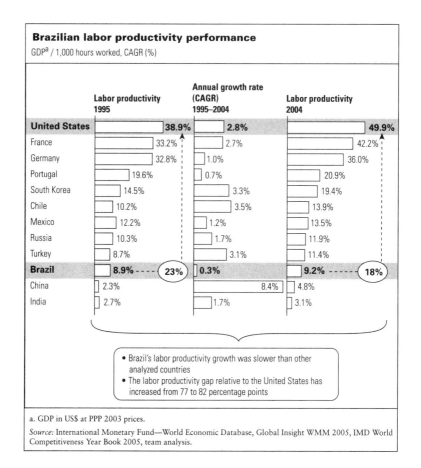

Brazilian labor productivity performance
GDP[a] / 1,000 hours worked, CAGR (%)

	Labor productivity 1995	Annual growth rate (CAGR) 1995–2004	Labor productivity 2004
United States	38.9%	2.8%	49.9%
France	33.2%	2.7%	42.2%
Germany	32.8%	1.0%	36.0%
Portugal	19.6%	0.7%	20.9%
South Korea	14.5%	3.3%	19.4%
Chile	10.2%	3.5%	13.9%
Mexico	12.2%	1.2%	13.5%
Russia	10.3%	1.7%	11.9%
Turkey	8.7%	3.1%	11.4%
Brazil	8.9% (23%)	0.3%	9.2% (18%)
China	2.3%	8.4%	4.8%
India	2.7%	1.7%	3.1%

- Brazil's labor productivity growth was slower than other analyzed countries
- The labor productivity gap relative to the United States has increased from 77 to 82 percentage points

a. GDP in US$ at PPP 2003 prices.

Source: International Monetary Fund—World Economic Database, Global Insight WMM 2005, IMD World Competitiveness Year Book 2005, team analysis.

development curve, and will work themselves out over time. The first of these is the fact that, because Brazil has a modest per capita income, consumers generally can only afford lower-priced products and services. This effectively acts as a brake on Brazil's development of home-grown higher value added production; the country produces mostly smaller, low-priced cars, for instance, relying on imports for more expensive models. The second issue is that, in Brazil, labor is cheap compared with capital, and this discourages the kind of capital investment that would boost productivity. However, neither of these characteristics need hold Brazilian productivity back in the longer term, as long as the economy achieves a healthier, sustained level of economic growth.

What matters most, however, are the nonstructural hurdles that are responsible for the remaining two-thirds of Brazil's productivity gap. Our analysis has found five primary barriers to raising productivity in Brazil: the large informal sector, macro-economic factors hampering investment, an onerous regulatory regime, and weaknesses in public service provision and the country's infrastructure (see "Barriers to productivity growth"). All of these could be tackled through adjustments to Brazil's social and economic policies. By far the most important of these, however, is the drag on productivity exerted by Brazil's informal sector.

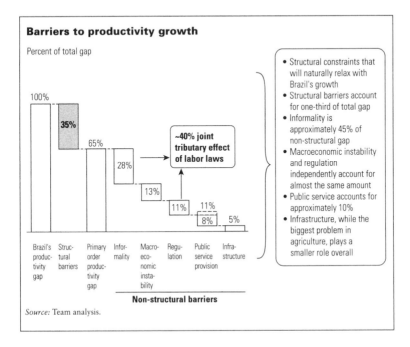

Barriers to productivity growth

Percent of total gap

- Structural constraints that will naturally relax with Brazil's growth
- Structural barriers account for one-third of total gap
- Informality is approximately 45% of non-structural gap
- Macroeconomic instability and regulation independently account for almost the same amount
- Public service accounts for approximately 10%
- Infrastructure, while the biggest problem in agriculture, plays a smaller role overall

Source: Team analysis.

Brazil's gray economy is biggest obstacle to productivity growth

Brazil's "gray" economy accounts for an estimated 40 percent of gross national income, making it far larger than those in other emerging markets. Having such a huge informal sector saddles Brazil's economy with a set of competitive and corporate distortions that profoundly compromise its prospects.[4] Our analysis shows that it explains 42 percent of the country's nonstructural productivity gap with the United States.

By avoiding taxes, ignoring quality and safety regulations, or infringing copyrights, gray market companies gain cost advantages that allow them to compete successfully against more efficient, law-abiding businesses. Honest companies lose market share, and thus make less money to invest in technology and other productivity-enhancing measures. Less efficient players tend to have a larger market share than they would have if they paid the taxes and labor fees they are supposed to.

In the Brazilian retail industry, a good example of a sector blighted by the gray economy, informal players enjoy higher margins than their formal competitors, and small and medium-sized enterprises, less productive than larger firms, derive an artificial advantage. In Brazil, small and medium-size retail outlets have a dominant 79 percent share of the retail market compared with 35 percent in the US equivalent. The result is far lower sales-per-employee (see "Comparison of sales per employee in medium/small formats in retail").

More labor tends to be retained in unproductive activities than is economically rational because it is artificially cheapened by tax and social security evasion. In Brazil's construction sector,

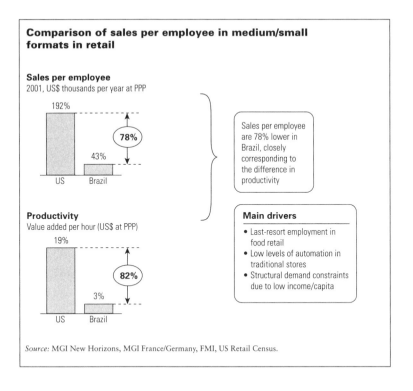

Comparison of sales per employee in medium/small formats in retail

Sales per employee
2001, US$ thousands per year at PPP

192%

78%

43%

US   Brazil

Sales per employee are 78% lower in Brazil, closely corresponding to the difference in productivity

Productivity
Value added per hour (US$ at PPP)

19%

82%

3%

US   Brazil

Main drivers
- Last-resort employment in food retail
- Low levels of automation in traditional stores
- Structural demand constraints due to low income/capita

Source: MGI New Horizons, MGI France/Germany, FMI, US Retail Census.

for instance, the percentage of those working in the informal economy increased from 61.3 percent in 1992 to 71.1 percent in 2002. Informality also discourages investment in automation and up-to-date equipment. There is no incentive for small, informal businesses to reach the scale required to innovate and adopt best practices because growing bigger increases the risk that the authorities will detect their informal practices.

Beating back the informal economy

Worryingly, Brazil's gray economy is not getting any smaller. The level of informal employment was virtually unchanged at about 55 percent from 1992 to 2002. This is despite the fact that, during this period, some 7 percent of the overall workforce migrated from agriculture, where the level of informality is around 90 percent. Instead of finding formal jobs in other sectors, these migrants substantially increased levels of informality in manufacturing, construction, and transportation. According to data on employment in Brazil's largest metropolitan regions, informal jobs accounted for 87 percent of all jobs created during this decade.

We estimate that Brazil's economy could grow by an additional 1.5 percent a year if the government emulated the successful measures of other countries, and launched a comprehensive program to fight informality.[5] In a six-year period during the 1990s, Spain implemented concerted reforms—including streamlining its tax system, strengthening auditing, and redesigning its public administration system—and achieved a 75 percent increase in taxes collected from businesses that had worked informally. Peru, which realized that many of its poor were effectively excluded from the formal sector by its extensive and complicated bureaucratic system, started addressing the issue in the early 1990s. For instance, the government made it less onerous to register a business—this now takes a single day instead of 300 previously, and costs $175 rather than $1,200. As a result, 671,000 companies and 558,000 jobs were formalized in Peru between 1991 and 1997.

Large informal sectors sprout up partly because of social and demographic trends—such as large-scale migration from rural to urban centers which can generate an excess of unskilled labor in towns. However, the critical reasons lie in government policy. Informality thrives when the cost of working formally is high and enforcement is weak; Brazil is a textbook example of both policy flaws.

According to the Institute for Management Development (IMD), the overall tax burden in Brazil increased from 26 percent of GDP in 1992 to 36 percent in 2002, effectively increasing the incentive for businesses to operate informally. Formal companies paid some two-thirds of all the taxes. In addition, Brazil has rigid and complex labor regulations, and onerous regulation of capital, product, and land markets. The sheer burden of complying with them all encourages businesses to avoid them, especially because the probability of being caught flouting them is not high—certainly not high enough to ensure compliance. Brazil has no specialized commercial courts, few tax collection agents, and a weak judiciary. For instance, the market share of illegally copied compact discs has been booming from 5 percent of the market in 1997 to 53 percent in 2002; yet, of 6,248 copyright-related lawsuits filed with the public attorney's office between 1999 and 2001, only 17 resulted in convictions.

Such policies make incentives to operate informally abnormally high in Brazil. In food retailing, for instance, a Brazilian supermarket can triple its income by evading taxes and social charges. In gasoline retailing, informality has been increasing rapidly as players seek to evade high gasoline taxes equivalent to almost half the pump price. Tax evasion in this sector may be worth more than 3.3 billion reais ($1.6 billion)—greater than all the petroleum royalties oil producers pay to Brazil's states and municipalities.

By contrast, Asian countries that have joined the ranks of the wealthy nations or dramatically narrowed the gap with them have never had a serious informality problem. Japan, Singapore, South Korea, and Taiwan all benefited from relatively small tax and regulatory burdens as well as from strong legal and law-enforcement systems. So did Western countries in the early stages of their development. The corporate tax burden was only 4 percent of GDP in the United States in 1913, when it was at Brazil's current stage of development; in present-day Brazil, corporate taxation is equivalent to nearly 25 percent of GDP.[6]

Further barriers to higher productivity

While tackling the gray economy should be Brazil's first priority, four further hurdles to higher productivity also deserve policymakers' close attention.

Macroeconomic factors

Despite improvements in macroeconomic management, business is still hobbled by a high degree of uncertainty about future exchange rates and interest rates. Executives therefore find it difficult to forecast demand for products and services, and are left with little choice but to focus on short-term financial management, rather than long-term growth and operating efficiency. Exporting industries such as automotive are particularly seriously hit by uncertainty over the future direction of exchange rates which prevents companies from choosing Brazil as an export base.

Economic uncertainty also discourages long-term investment—such as automation—as companies and investors demand higher returns to compensate for macroeconomic risks. The result is that Brazil's interest rates are high—8 percent, compared with just 2.7 percent in the United States—and the market for long-term debt is virtually nonexistent. Sectors such as residential construction, which relies on consumer credit, are hampered by the embryonic nature of Brazil's capital markets and therefore the limitations on mortgage finance. McKinsey estimates that macroeconomic uncertainty accounts for 20 percent of the productivity deficit produced by our five primary barriers.

Regulatory constraints

Brazil's complex, bureaucratic regulatory regime accounts for another 17 per cent of the nonstructural productivity gap, according to our estimates. Our understanding of regulations covers the gamut from labor and tax laws, to price controls, product regulations, trade barriers, and subsidies. Regulatory constraints on productivity are particularly marked in non-tradable, capital-intensive sectors such as retail banking and telecoms.

Labor laws. Brazil's labor legislation is rigid, particularly in comparison with the United States, and this significantly constrains productivity. The thorniest problem for businesses is limits on hiring and firing workers. This leaves them vulnerable to fluctuations in demand, particularly in highly cyclical sectors such as residential construction. The high cost of laying workers off encourages informal employment. All too many employers find this route attractive because it allows them to avoid paying expensive payroll taxes, and gives them the flexibility—not available in the formal sector—to manage their workforces. Labor market rigidity, which affects all the industries we studied, is clearly hampering the ability of Brazilian companies to optimize their operations and create new jobs, and deters direct foreign investment in Brazil.

Tax regulation. High taxes drive costs up and demand down. For instance, the actual cost of making similar vehicles in the

United States and Brazil is about the same; but add in Brazil's sales taxes, and prices rise significantly across the entire Brazilian manufacturing chain to the detriment of the final consumer. High prices not only reduce overall demand for new vehicles, but also the average value of automobiles sold in Brazil.

Regulatory complexity and bureaucracy. Brazil labors under a web of city, state, and federal taxes and regulations that hinder entrepreneurialism and make it difficult for the financial system to function. For instance, in the residential construction sector, standards are imposed that are prescriptive and not performance-based. For instance, they will stipulate how thick a wall must be, but say nothing about the structural resistance or thermal and acoustic insulation it should provide. These imposed standards tend to delay the incorporation of innovative construction with superior properties. For example, drywall, widely used in the United States, has very low penetration in Brazil.

Subsidies and barriers to free trade. Productivity is compromised by a panoply of regulations that hamper free trade, including prohibition on the entry of new competitors into a particular market, tariff protections, and subsidies that favor some players over others.

State-owned businesses. Government-owned businesses overall boast lower productivity than companies in the private sector. In the retail banking sector, for instance, state-controlled banks own 37 percent of all the assets of the banking system and account for 40 percent of its employment. This drags down the productivity of the sector as a whole. The cost efficiency of Brazil's commercial banking sector—measured as a cost-to-income ratio—improved between 1997 and 2002, dropping from 80.1 to 70.8. But the ratio among US banks fell from 60 to 55 over the same period, leaving Brazil's banks still far behind. The productivity of Brazil's publicly owned banks is only just over half of the country's leading private bank.

Public-sector weaknesses

Inefficient public services account, we estimate, for up to 11 percent of the primary barriers to Brazilian productivity growth that we identified. Public services are responsible for 11 percent of total employment in the country. They do not deliver effectively, and that holds the private sector back. For instance, one-quarter of the population receives no secondary schooling; almost 12 percent of adults—some 15 million people—cannot read or write. This impedes the adoption and use of innovative new products and techniques in sectors such as agriculture.

Infrastructural weaknesses

Finally, Brazil has a significant infrastructure deficit with inadequate highways, ports, railroads, and power generation and storage facilities (see "Comparison of Brazilian vs. US infrastructure"). McKinsey estimates that this accounts for 5 percent of the primary barriers to greater productivity. In agriculture, for instance, up to 12 percent of all grain produced in Brazil spoils before reaching ports or the end consumer. Freight costs and port tariffs for Brazil's soybean producers are $16 a ton or 55 percent higher than the equivalent costs for their US

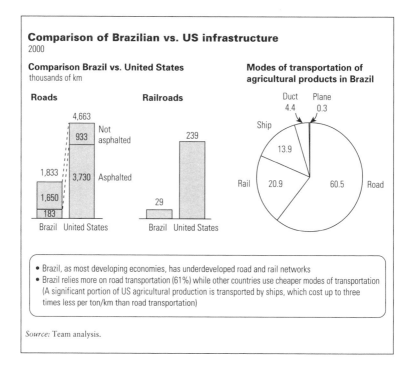

Comparison of Brazilian vs. US infrastructure
2000

Comparison Brazil vs. United States
thousands of km

Modes of transportation of agricultural products in Brazil

Roads / Railroads / Pie chart values: Duct 4.4, Plane 0.3, Ship, Rail 20.9, Road 60.5, 13.9

- Brazil, as most developing economies, has underdeveloped road and rail networks
- Brazil relies more on road transportation (61%) while other countries use cheaper modes of transportation (A significant portion of US agricultural production is transported by ships, which cost up to three times less per ton/km than road transportation)

Source: Team analysis.

competitors, reducing their margins on international prices by 10 percent. Costs in Brazil's automotive industry are raised by factors including relatively expensive transportation and long waiting times at dockside, which cause expensive build-ups of inventory.

The way forward

The barriers to improving productivity in Brazil's economy are formidably deep-seated. Dismantling them is bound to be hard work. But there is much cause for optimism. In our experience, once the sources of low productivity are identified, there is no impediment to governments adopting a program of long-term structural and economic adjustment.

Take the informality barrier. The government of Brazil has started to undertake key structural reforms that will tackle this problem—passing public pension and tax bills and legislation to modernizing bankruptcy law. Predominantly informal sectors—such as retailing and construction—will require even more tailored, structural changes. By tackling informality sector by sector, and tailoring the approach, policymakers will be able to deliver the kind of quick wins that generate the political momentum required for further change. For instance, the federal tax collection agency now requires leak-measurement devices in all Brazilian beverage plants—a move that could quickly cut by some 70 percent the sector's estimated annual tax evasion of 720 million reais, or $360m.

Brazil also needs to tighten up its legal system, and consider following the lead of other countries such as Ireland and the Netherlands in creating a special agency to fight evasion of taxes and social charges. More fundamentally, it should consider lowering the burden of both taxation and regulation—so that informality doesn't pay.

Such measures, along with policies to tackle Brazil's other major productivity barriers, have succeeded elsewhere. The government of the Republic of Ireland, for instance, transformed the country's economic prospects and performance within a relatively short time scale by embracing a well-articulated strategy to dismantle the kind of barriers we have found in Brazil.

Two-thirds of Brazil's productivity deficit can be tackled by changes in government policy. The rest will come when the economy moves onto a sustainable, healthy growth track. There is all to play for.

Heinz-Peter Elstrodt, Jorge A. Fergie, and Martha A. Laboissière, *McKinsey Quarterly,* 2006 Number 2.

Notes

1. See Goldman Sachs Global Economics Paper 99 "Dreaming with BRICS: The Path to 2050," October 2003.

2. See, for example, the OECD's Economic Survey of Brazil 2005 at www.oecd.org.

3. See "Productivity: The key to an accelerated development path for Brazil," MGI, March 1998, at www. Mckinsey.com/mgi/ and Martin N. Baily et al., "Will Brazil seize its future?" *The McKinsey Quarterly,* 1998, Number 3.

4. See Diana Farrell, "The hidden dangers of the informal economy," *The McKinsey Quarterly,* 2004 Number 3.

5. See "Reining in Brazil's informal economy," *The McKinsey Quarterly,* Web exclusive, January 2005 at www.mckinseyquarterly .com for more details of reforms to curb the informal sector.

6. See Bill Lewis, *The Power of Productivity,* University of Chicago Press, 2004.

Index

About the Authors

The power of productivity

William W. Lewis, a McKinsey alumnus, was the founding director of the McKinsey Global Institute. This article was adapted from chapter 1 of his new book, *The Power of Productivity: Wealth, Poverty, and the Threat to Global Stability* (Chicago: University of Chicago Press, 2004).

Regulation that's good for competition

Scott C. Beardsley is a director in the McKinsey Brussels office, and **Diana Farrell** is the director of the McKinsey Global Institute.

What's right with the US economy

William W. Lewis, a McKinsey alumnus, was the founding director of the McKinsey Global Institute. **Vincent Palmade** is an alumnus from McKinsey's Washington, D.C., office and MGI. **Baudouin Regout** is an associate principal in McKinsey's Brussels office. **Allen P. Webb** is a senior editor at the *McKinsey Quarterly.*

Reviving French and German productivity

Diana Farrell is the director of the McKinsey Global Institute. **Heino Fassbender** is a director emeritus from McKinsey's Frankfurt office. **Thomas Kneip** is an alumnus from McKinsey's Munich office. **Stephan Kriesel** is an associate principal in McKinsey's Dubai office. **Eric Labaye** is a director in McKinsey's Paris office.

Sweden's golden opportunity

Kalle Bengtsson is a principal and **Claes Ekström** is a director in McKinsey's Stockholm office; **Martin Hjerpe** is a senior economist with McKinsey.

Turkey's quest for stable growth

Didem Dincer Baser is an alumnus from McKinsey's Istanbul office, where David Meen is a director emeritus. Diana Farrell is the director of the McKinsey Global Institute.

Asia: The productivity imperative

Diana Farrell is the director of the McKinsey Global Institute.

China and India: The race to growth

Jayant Sinha is an alumnus from McKinsey's New Delhi office. Tarun Khanna is the Jorge Paulo Lemann professor at the Harvard Business School. Jonathan R. Woetzel is a director in McKinsey's Shanghai office. Diana Farrell is the director of the McKinsey Global Institute.

India: From emerging to surging

Amadeo Di Lodovico is a principal in McKinsey's Caracas office. William W. Lewis, a McKinsey alumnus, was the founding director of the McKinsey Global Institute. Vincent Palmade is an alumnus of McKinsey's Washington, DC office and MGI. Shirish Sankhe is a principal in McKinsey's Mumbai office.

A richer future for India

Diana Farrell is the director of the McKinsey Global Institute, and Adil S. Zainulbhai is a director in McKinsey's Mumbai office.

How Brazil can grow

Heinz-Peter Elstrodt and Jorge A. Fergie are directors in McKinsey's São Paulo office, and Martha A. Laboissière is a senior fellow at the McKinsey Global Institute.